202 Amazing Microwave Recipes

(202 Amazing Microwave Recipes - Volume 1)

Mary Solomon

Content

202 Awesome Microwave Recipes

***

1. A Versatile Green Broccoli Rabe Pasta Sauce

Serving: 6 first-course servings | Prep: | Cook: |Ready in: 20mins

Ingredients

- 1 ½ pounds broccoli rabe, trimmed and cut across into 1-inch pieces
- 6 tablespoons olive oil
- 1 teaspoon crushed red-pepper flakes
- 1 teaspoon salt
- Freshly ground black pepper to taste

Direction

- Place the broccoli rabe in a five-quart casserole. Toss with the olive oil and crushed red-pepper flakes.
- Cover tightly with microwave plastic wrap. Cook at 100 percent power in a high-power oven for 10 minutes. Prick plastic to release steam.
- Remove from oven and uncover. Season with salt and freshly ground black pepper to taste. Toss with cooked and drained pasta.

Nutrition Information

- 146: calories;
- 4 grams: protein;
- 3 grams: dietary fiber;
- 0 grams: sugars;
- 296 milligrams: sodium;
- 14 grams: fat;

- 2 grams: polyunsaturated fat;
- 10 grams: monounsaturated fat;

2. All American Stewed Tomatoes

Serving: 6 cups | Prep: | Cook: |Ready in: 30mins

Ingredients

- 4 tablespoons butter
- ¼ cup sugar
- 2 teaspoons kosher salt
- 4 slices fresh ginger, about the size of a quarter, peeled and julienned
- ¼ teaspoon paprika
- Pinch ground cloves
- ¼ pound yellow onion, peeled, halved and thinly sliced
- 3 pounds ripe tomatoes, cored and cut into 1-inch wedges
- 2 tablespoons cornstarch dissolved in 1/4-cup water
- 2 tablespoons fresh lemon juice
- Freshly ground black pepper

Direction

- In a glass or ceramic dish (11 by 14 by 2 inches), combine butter, sugar, salt, ginger, paprika, cloves and onion. Cook, uncovered, at 100 percent for 4 minutes.
- Stir in tomatoes. Push tomatoes to the edge of the dish so that they make a ring, leaving an open area in the center. Cover dish tightly with polyvinyl microwave plastic wrap. Cook at 100 percent for 8 minutes. Pierce plastic and stir in dissolved cornstarch. Patch plastic. Cook at 100 percent for 3 minutes longer.
- Prick plastic. Uncover carefully. Stir in lemon juice and pepper to taste. Serve immediately.

Nutrition Information

- 163: calories;
- 8 grams: fat;
- 5 grams: saturated fat;
- 2 grams: protein;
- 3 grams: dietary fiber;
- 15 grams: sugars;
- 635 milligrams: sodium;
- 0 grams: polyunsaturated fat;
- 23 grams: carbohydrates;

3. Amaretti Apple Crisp

Serving: 6 servings | Prep: | Cook: | Ready in: 20mins

Ingredients

- 4 Granny Smith apples (7 ounces each), peeled, cored and cut into 1-inch pieces
- ¼ cup fresh lemon juice
- 1 ½ teaspoons cornstarch
- 5 tablespoons light brown sugar
- 1 teaspoon almond extract
- ¼ teaspoon ground nutmeg
- ⅛ teaspoon ground cloves
- 1 cup slivered almonds
- 2 tablespoons sweet butter
- 3 ounces amaretti cookies

Direction

- Place apples in an 8-by-8-by-2-inch glass or ceramic baking dish. Add 3 tablespoons of the lemon juice, and toss to combine.
- Place the cornstarch in a very small bowl. Stir in 1 tablespoon of the lemon juice. Stir in remaining 2 teaspoons lemon juice, 2 tablespoons of the brown sugar and the almond extract, nutmeg and cloves.
- Add the cornstarch mixture and almonds to the apples, and toss to combine. Cover tightly with microwave plastic wrap. Cook at 100 percent power in a high-power oven for 7 minutes, stirring once. Then prick the plastic to release steam.

- Remove from the oven, uncover and set aside. Preheat the broiler.
- Place the butter in a 1-cup glass measure. Cook, uncovered, for 1 minute, then remove from the oven.
- Place the butter, amaretti and remaining brown sugar in a food processor. Process until finely chopped. Sprinkle over the apples, and brown under broiler for about 3 minutes.

Nutrition Information

- 306: calories;
- 5 grams: protein;
- 15 grams: fat;
- 4 grams: saturated fat;
- 0 grams: trans fat;
- 8 grams: monounsaturated fat;
- 39 grams: carbohydrates;
- 6 grams: dietary fiber;
- 3 grams: polyunsaturated fat;
- 23 grams: sugars;
- 62 milligrams: sodium;

4. Apricot Jellies

Serving: 280 3/4-inch squares | Prep: | Cook: | Ready in: 1hours

Ingredients

- 2 pounds dried apricots
- 3 cups water
- 4 ½ cups granulated sugar
- Vegetable oil for coating pan

Direction

- Place apricots and water in a 2 1/2-quart souffle dish with a tight lid. Cook, covered, at 100 percent power in a high-power microwave oven for 12 minutes, stirring once.
- Remove from oven. Transfer apricots and liquid to a food processor. Process until

smooth, stopping once to scrape sides of bowl. Add 3 cups of the sugar in two batches; process until smooth after each addition, stopping to scrape sides and stir sugar down into the puree.

- Scrape mixture back into souffle dish. Cook, uncovered, for 30 minutes, stirring well three times.
- Remove from oven. Oil a 10 1/2-by-15 1/2-inch jellyroll pan. Scrape mixture into pan and smooth with a spatula. Refrigerate until firm enough to cut, 3 hours or overnight.
- Place remaining sugar in a small bowl. Rinse a knife with hot water. Cut candy into 3/4-inch squares, rinsing the knife from time to time as you lift squares from pan. Coat each square on all sides in the sugar. As they are coated, place on a cake rack. Let stand overnight, until dry.

5. Apricot Poached Pears

Serving: 4 servings | Prep: | Cook: | Ready in: 18mins

Ingredients

- ½ cup apricot preserves
- 3 tablespoons fresh lemon juice
- 1 tablespoon kirsch
- 4 Bosc pears
- 4 dried apricots

Direction

- Put preserves in a 1-cup measure. Cook, uncovered, at 100 percent power in a high-power oven for 1 minute. Remove from oven.
- Stir in 1 tablespoon of the lemon juice and the kirsch. Pass mixture through a sieve into a shallow bowl. Set aside.
- Peel the pears and core them through the bottom. As you work, rub the pears inside and out with the remaining lemon juice to prevent discoloration.

- Roll each apricot lengthwise and put one in the cavity of each pear. Coat the pears in the apricot mixture.
- Arrange pears in a circle around the inside rim of a 2 1/4-quart souffle dish. Cover tightly with microwave plastic wrap. Cook 7 minutes. Prick plastic to release steam.
- Remove from oven and uncover. Serve hot or cold. Put each pear on a plate and spoon some of the remaining sauce over.

Nutrition Information

- 249: calories;
- 1 gram: protein;
- 19 milligrams: sodium;
- 0 grams: polyunsaturated fat;
- 61 grams: carbohydrates;
- 7 grams: dietary fiber;
- 41 grams: sugars;

6. Apricot Steamed Pudding

Serving: 8 servings | Prep: | Cook: | Ready in: 1hours

Ingredients

- 1 cup dried apricots
- 1 cup granulated sugar
- 2 tablespoons fresh lemon juice
- 1 stick plus 1 tablespoon unsalted butter, cut in small pieces
- 2 large eggs
- 2 cups very fine, fresh white bread crumbs (from 5 slices of bread)

Direction

- In a 1 1/2-quart glass or ceramic souffle dish, stir together the apricots, 1 cup water and 1/2 cup sugar. Cover tightly with microwave plastic wrap. Cook at 100 percent power for 7 minutes. Prick plastic wrap to release steam.

- Remove from oven, and uncover. Scrape mixture into a blender, and puree. Scrape down sides of blender. Add lemon juice, and blend until smooth. Put puree into a medium bowl, and let stand 15 minutes or until cool.
- Place a 2-quart souffle dish on parchment paper. Lightly trace around the base with a pencil. Cut out the paper disk just inside the pencil marking. Grease the dish and both sides of the paper using 1 tablespoon of the butter.
- Place the remaining sugar and butter in the work bowl of a food processor, and process until smooth. With processor running, add the eggs one at a time to combine. Add the apricot puree, and process until completely incorporated.
- Return apricot mixture to the bowl, and gently fold in the bread crumbs until well combined. Pour the mixture into the prepared souffle dish. To remove the air bubbles, firmly rap dish on counter. Cover tightly with microwave plastic wrap. Cook 12 minutes. Prick plastic to release steam.
- Remove from the oven, and uncover. Cover with a heavy plate, and let stand for 15 minutes. Unmold; remove parchment paper, let cool about 5 minutes and serve.

Nutrition Information

- 375: calories;
- 1 gram: polyunsaturated fat;
- 4 grams: monounsaturated fat;
- 219 milligrams: sodium;
- 16 grams: fat;
- 9 grams: saturated fat;
- 6 grams: protein;
- 55 grams: carbohydrates;
- 2 grams: dietary fiber;
- 35 grams: sugars;

7. Artichoke Bottoms With White Wine Duxelles

Serving: 4 servings as garnish, 2 servings as first course | Prep: | Cook: | Ready in: 26mins

Ingredients

- 4 artichokes, cooked as above
- ¼ cup fresh lemon juice
- 2 tablespoons butter
- 2 shallots, peeled and minced
- ¼ pound mushrooms, stems removed, caps finely diced
- 1 small plum tomato, cored, seeded and chopped
- ⅓ cup white wine
- 2 tablespoons minced parsley
- ½ teaspoon kosher salt
- Freshly ground black pepper

Direction

- Peel leaves from artichokes. Remove chokes with a spoon and discard. Trim bottoms so the edges are smooth. If necessary cut small slices from stem ends so the artichokes will sit upright. Rub all over with lemon juice to prevent discoloration.
- In a 10-inch ceramic quiche dish heat the butter, uncovered, at 100 percent power for 1 minute in a large oven, or 2 minutes 30 seconds in a small oven. Add shallots, mushrooms and tomato and stir. Cook, uncovered, at 100 percent power for 3 minutes in a large oven, or 4 minutes and 30 seconds in a small oven.
- Add the wine. Cook, uncovered, at 100 percent power for 5 minutes in a large oven, or 8 minutes in a small one, until most of the wine has evaporated. Remove from oven. Stir in parsley, salt and pepper.
- Set artichoke bottoms in a circle on a 10-inch platter. Mound a quarter of the mushroom mixture in the well of each artichoke. Heat, uncovered, at 100 percent power for 2 minutes

in a large oven or 3 minutes in a small one. Serve immediately.

Nutrition Information

- 121: calories;
- 284 milligrams: sodium;
- 6 grams: fat;
- 4 grams: sugars;
- 0 grams: polyunsaturated fat;
- 2 grams: monounsaturated fat;
- 13 grams: carbohydrates;
- 3 grams: protein;

8. Artichoke Hazelnut Soup

Serving: 4 cups, or 4 to 6 servings | Prep: | Cook: | Ready in: 29mins

Ingredients

- 6 artichokes, cooked as above
- 2 tablespoons fresh lemon juice
- ⅓ pound hazelnuts
- 2 cups fresh or canned chicken broth (see note)
- ½ cup heavy cream
- 2 tablespoons kosher salt
- Freshly ground black pepper

Direction

- Peel leaves from artichokes. Remove chokes with a spoon and discard. In a food processor, puree the artichoke bottoms with lemon juice until smooth. Reserve.
- Spread the hazelnuts in one layer in a 10-inch round dish. Cook, uncovered, at 100 percent power 7 minutes in a large oven, or 9 minutes in a small oven. Pour the hazelnuts onto a clean kitchen towel, fold it over and rub until most of the skins are removed. Process the nuts in a food processor or blender until finely ground.

- In an 8-cup glass measure whisk together the artichoke puree, ground nuts, broth and cream. Season with salt and pepper.
- Heat, uncovered, at 100 percent power 6 minutes, stirring twice.

Nutrition Information

- 254: calories;
- 410 milligrams: sodium;
- 6 grams: protein;
- 5 grams: dietary fiber;
- 3 grams: sugars;
- 23 grams: fat;
- 14 grams: monounsaturated fat;
- 2 grams: polyunsaturated fat;
- 10 grams: carbohydrates;

9. Artichokes With Caviar Sauce

Serving: 2 servings | Prep: | Cook: | Ready in: 25mins

Ingredients

- 2 artichokes (10 ounces each)
- ½ fresh lemon
- ½ cup mayonnaise
- 1 tablespoon brandy
- 1 tablespoon water
- 2 teaspoons fresh lemon juice
- Freshly ground black pepper to taste
- 1 ounce salmon roe
- 1 tablespoon snipped chives

Direction

- With a serrated knife, cut off the top 1 1/2 inches of each artichoke. Cut or break off the stems flush with the bottoms and remove the outer two rows of leaves. Rub cut surfaces with the lemon half as you work. Place the trimmed artichokes in a glass or ceramic dish large enough to hold them without touching. Cover tightly with microwave plastic wrap.

Cook at 100 percent power in a high-power oven for 10 minutes. Prick plastic to release steam.

- Remove from oven and uncover. Cover the dish with a damp cloth until artichokes are cool enough to handle. Push down on the leaves to make a flower shape and to expose the pale center leaves covering the fuzzy choke. Pull out the cone of center leaves, and with a small spoon, scrape out the choke. Allow to cool. Cover tightly, and refrigerate until ready to serve.
- Whisk together the mayonnaise, brandy, water, lemon juice and pepper until smooth. Stir in salmon roe and chives. Refrigerate until cold.
- Place each artichoke bottom on a plate. Spoon some of the sauce into the heart and around each artichoke, and serve.

Nutrition Information

- 496: calories;
- 454 milligrams: sodium;
- 46 grams: fat;
- 7 grams: protein;
- 11 grams: monounsaturated fat;
- 27 grams: polyunsaturated fat;
- 15 grams: carbohydrates;
- 2 grams: sugars;

---

10. Asian Marinated Eggplant

Serving: 4 side-dish servings | Prep: | Cook: | Ready in: 18mins

Ingredients

- ¼ cup tamari
- 2 tablespoons loosely packed cilantro leaves
- 1 tablespoon rice-wine vinegar
- 1 teaspoon toasted sesame oil
- 1 ½ medium-size cloves garlic, smashed and peeled

- ⅜ ounce peeled fresh ginger (a 1-by- 1/4-inch piece), cut crosswise into 1/4-inch slices
- 4 medium-size Chinese eggplants (2 ounces each)

Direction

- Combine all ingredients, except eggplants, in a blender. Process until smooth.
- Prick the eggplants several times with a fork and pull off the leaves. Cut in half lengthwise. On the open side of each half, make three deep diagonal slashes in each direction. Place eggplants skin side down in a 13-by-9-by-2-inch oval dish.
- Spoon 1 1/2 teaspoons of the marinade over each eggplant half. Rub the marinade into the flesh so that it runs into the cuts. Turn eggplants skin side up. Pour remaining marinade into dish. Let stand for 45 minutes.
- Turn eggplants skin side down. Cover tightly with microwave plastic wrap. Cook at 100 percent power in a high-power oven for 10 minutes. Prick plastic to release steam.
- Remove from oven and uncover. Spoon sauce over eggplants.

Nutrition Information

- 37: calories;
- 1 gram: polyunsaturated fat;
- 0 grams: monounsaturated fat;
- 5 grams: carbohydrates;
- 2 grams: protein;
- 1008 milligrams: sodium;

---

11. Baked Bean And Cheese Quesadillas

Serving: One serving | Prep: | Cook: | Ready in: 5mins

Ingredients

- For the baked bean and cheese quesadillas

- 2 corn tortillas
- ⅓ cup cooked baked beans, homemade or canned, with sauce
- 1 ounce grated Monterey Jack, Cheddar or mixed cheeses 1/4 cup
- Salsa for serving optional

Direction

- In a microwave: Place a corn tortilla on a plate. Top with the beans. Lightly mash the beans with the back of a spoon. Sprinkle on the cheese, and top with the remaining tortilla. Press down gently, then microwave for 1 to 1 1/2 minutes until the cheese has melted. Remove from the microwave, cut into quarters or sixths and serve.
- In a pan: Place a corn tortilla in a pan. Top with the beans. Lightly mash the beans with the back of a spoon. Sprinkle on the cheese. Turn the heat to medium-high, and heat until the cheese begins to melt. Place the remaining tortilla on top of the cheese, and press down lightly. Flip over the quesadilla in the pan, and heat for about 30 seconds or until the cheese has melted. Flip back over, and remove to a plate. Cut into quarters or sixths and serve.

Nutrition Information

- 289: calories;
- 10 grams: fat;
- 6 grams: dietary fiber;
- 1 gram: polyunsaturated fat;
- 40 grams: carbohydrates;
- 7 grams: sugars;
- 14 grams: protein;
- 482 milligrams: sodium;
- 3 grams: monounsaturated fat;

12. Barbara Kafka's Lemon Curd

Serving: 3 cups | Prep: | Cook: | Ready in: 24mins

Ingredients

- ½ pound unsalted butter
- 1 cup granulated sugar
- ½ cup fresh lemon juice
- 1 tablespoon finely grated or chopped lemon zest (of 2 lemons)
- 2 tablespoons finely grated or chopped orange zest, optional
- 6 large eggs

Direction

- Place butter, sugar, lemon juice and zests in an 8-cup glass measure or a 2 1/2-quart souffle dish. Cover tightly with microwave plastic wrap. Cook at 100 percent power in a 650- to 700-watt oven for 4 minutes. Prick plastic to release steam.
- Remove from oven and uncover. Whisk together eggs in a small bowl. Whisk about 1/4 cup of the butter mixture into the eggs to warm them. Scrape egg mixture back into measure, whisking constantly. Cook uncovered for 3 minutes.
- Leaving dish in oven, whisk until smooth. Cook, uncovered, for 2 minutes more. Remove from oven and puree in a food processor or blender until completely smooth. Store, tightly covered, in the refrigerator for up to 2 weeks.

Nutrition Information

- 238: calories;
- 18 grams: carbohydrates;
- 10 grams: saturated fat;
- 1 gram: polyunsaturated fat;
- 5 grams: monounsaturated fat;
- 0 grams: dietary fiber;
- 17 grams: sugars;
- 3 grams: protein;
- 38 milligrams: sodium;

13. Barbecued Chicken And Mushroom Tostadas

Serving: 4 servings. | Prep: | Cook: | Ready in: 45mins

Ingredients

- 1 whole chicken breast on the bone, skinned and split, or 2 boneless, skinless chicken breasts, 1 1/3 to 1 1/2 pounds
- 2 ½ quarts water
- 1 onion, quartered
- 2 garlic cloves, peeled and crushed
- ½ teaspoon dried thyme or oregano, or a combination
- Salt to taste
- 1 tablespoon extra virgin olive oil
- 8 white or cremini mushrooms, trimmed and sliced
- ¼ cup prepared barbecue sauce
- 6 corn tortillas, halved and toasted in the microwave (see above)
- 2 cups arugula
- 1 to 2 tablespoons fresh lime juice
- 6 radishes

Direction

-
-
-

Nutrition Information

- 218: calories;
- 6 grams: fat;
- 1 gram: polyunsaturated fat;
- 0 grams: trans fat;
- 29 grams: carbohydrates;
- 4 grams: dietary fiber;
- 3 grams: monounsaturated fat;
- 9 grams: sugars;
- 13 grams: protein;
- 1821 milligrams: sodium;

14. Barley Risotto With Rabe

Serving: 8 cups | Prep: | Cook: | Ready in: 1hours10mins

Ingredients

- ½ cup olive oil
- 1 medium-size onion, minced
- 8 large garlic cloves, smashed, peeled and minced
- 2 cups medium-size pearl barley
- 5 ½ cups chicken broth or vegetarian broth (see Micro-Tip)
- 1 pound broccoli rabe, trimmed and cut in 1/2-inch pieces
- 2 teaspoons kosher salt
- Freshly ground black pepper to tast

Direction

- Place oil in an oval dish, 14 by 9 by 2 inches. Cook, uncovered, at 100 percent in a high-power oven for 2 minutes. Stir in onion and garlic. Cook for 4 minutes. Stir in barley. Cook for 2 minutes.
- Stir in broth. Cook for 15 minutes. Stir in rabe. Cook for 25 minutes.
- Remove from oven. Cover with a towel and let stand for 10 minutes. Stir in salt and pepper.

Nutrition Information

- 249: calories;
- 31 grams: carbohydrates;
- 1 gram: sugars;
- 7 grams: protein;
- 417 milligrams: sodium;
- 12 grams: fat;
- 2 grams: polyunsaturated fat;
- 8 grams: dietary fiber;

15. Basic Polenta

Serving: 10 servings | Prep: | Cook: | Ready in: 17mins

Ingredients

- 4 cups water (add 1/4 cup if using a coarse polenta grind)
- 1 ¼ cups yellow or white cornmeal (American or coarse polenta grind)
- 2 teaspoons kosher salt
- 3 tablespoons unsalted butter (add 1 tablespoon if chilling for polenta lasagna)
- Pinch freshly ground black pepper

Direction

- Combine water, cornmeal and salt in a 2 1/2-quart souffle dish. Cook, uncovered, at 100 percent power in a 650- to 700-watt oven for 12 minutes, stirring once.
- Remove from oven. Stir in 3 tablespoons of the butter and the pepper. Serve; if making the polenta lasagna, proceed to step 3.
- Use 1 1/2 teaspoons of the butter to grease a 14-by-11-by-2-inch dish or a baking sheet. Pour the polenta mixture into the dish or spread it 1/2 inch thick in an even rectangle on the baking sheet. Smooth the top with a spatula, and spread the remaining 1 1/2 teaspoons of butter on top. Let stand until cool. Refrigerate overnight or until thoroughly chilled. With a sharp knife, cut the polenta crosswise into 10 equal rectangles. Leave the slices in dish or on the baking sheet until ready to use.

Nutrition Information

- 103: calories;
- 4 grams: fat;
- 2 grams: saturated fat;
- 0 grams: sugars;
- 1 gram: protein;
- 16 grams: carbohydrates;
- 276 milligrams: sodium;

16. Bean Tostadas

Serving: 4 to 6 servings | Prep: | Cook: | Ready in: 15mins

Ingredients

- ½ batch refried black beans or refried pinto beans (use same method for pintos as for black beans) (about 2 cups)
- 8 corn tortillas, halved and toasted in the microwave
- 1 medium or large avocado, mashed and seasoned with lime juice, salt, garlic if desired, cumin and chili (chopped fresh or powder)
- ⅓ cup crumbled queso fresco (about 1 1/2 ounces)
- 3 or 4 leaves romaine lettuce, cut in chiffonade
- ½ to 1 cup salsa, fresh or bottled
- Cilantro leaves for garnish

Direction

- Warm the refried beans in a 325-degree oven while you toast the tortilla halves. If the refried beans are too thick to spread evenly, thin out with some bean broth. Spread a spoonful of the refried beans onto each tortilla half. Top with a spoonful of the mashed avocado mixture and a sprinkle of queso fresco. Add a handful of lettuce and a spoonful of salsa. Arrange on a platter or plates and serve.

Nutrition Information

- 107: calories;
- 2 grams: sugars;
- 4 grams: protein;
- 298 milligrams: sodium;
- 3 grams: dietary fiber;
- 1 gram: polyunsaturated fat;
- 0 grams: trans fat;
- 18 grams: carbohydrates;

17. Belgian Carp Stew

Serving: 4 to 6 servings (about 6 cups) | Prep: | Cook: | Ready in: 59mins

Ingredients

- ¾ pound carp bones and heads, washed and cut into 2-inch pieces
- 2 bottles Belgian beer
- 5 tablespoons cold unsalted butter, cut into small pieces
- ½ pound mushrooms, wiped clean, trimmed and cut across into thin slices
- 4 shallots, peeled and cut across into thin slices (1/2 cup)
- 2 ribs celery, peeled and cut into fine julienne (3/4 cup)
- 1 tablespoon chopped fresh parsley
- 1 ½ pounds carp fillets, cut across into 1-inch wide strips
- 1 cup heavy cream
- 2 egg yolks
- 1 ½ teaspoons kosher salt
- Freshly ground black pepper, to taste

Direction

- Place fish bones and heads in a 2 1/2-quart souffle dish with a tight-fitting lid and pour beer over top. Cover with lid and cook in a 650- to 700-watt oven at 100 percent power for 15 minutes. Remove lid and cook for 5 minutes longer.
- Remove from oven and uncover. Strain broth through a fine sieve. Discard solids and reserve broth, there should be about 1 3/4 cups; add water if needed to make 1 3/4 cups.
- In same souffle dish, place 1 tablespoon butter and cook, uncovered, at 100 percent power for 1 minute. Remove from oven and stir in mushrooms, shallots, celery, and parsley. Cover with lid and cook at 100 percent power for 3 minutes.
- Remove from oven and uncover. Stir in fish and add reserved broth. Cover with lid and cook at 100 percent power for 5 minutes.
- Remove from oven and uncover. With a slotted spoon remove all solids to a bowl and reserve the cooking liquid in the dish. In a medium-size bowl whisk together cream and egg yolks. Gradually whisk in about 1 cup of cooking liquid. Whisk mixture back into souffle dish. Cover with lid and cook at 100 percent power for 5 minutes, stirring once during cooking.
- Remove from oven and uncover. Whisk in remaining butter until melted and season with salt and pepper. Return fish and vegetables to souffle dish and serve.

Nutrition Information

- 525: calories;
- 1 gram: dietary fiber;
- 34 grams: protein;
- 592 milligrams: sodium;
- 10 grams: carbohydrates;
- 3 grams: sugars;
- 35 grams: fat;
- 18 grams: saturated fat;
- 0 grams: trans fat;
- 11 grams: monounsaturated fat;
- 4 grams: polyunsaturated fat;

18. Black Bean Chili

Serving: 9 cups | Prep: | Cook: | Ready in: 50mins

Ingredients

- for beans:
- ¼ cup vegetable oil
- 1 large onion, peeled and chopped
- 10 medium garlic cloves, smashed, peeled and chopped
- 2 tablespoons ground cumin
- 1 eggplant, cut in 1/4-inch dice

- 1 medium red bell pepper, stemmed, seeded, deribbed and cut in 1/4-inch dice
- 4 to 4 ½ jalapeno peppers, stemmed, seeded, deribbed and minced
- 3 medium zucchini, cut in 1/4-inch dice
- 2 cups black beans, cooked (see Micro-Tip) or 4 1/2 cups canned black beans, drained and rinsed
- 1 (28-ounce can) tomatoes, drained and coarsely chopped (liquid reserved)
- 2 bunches coriander, chopped
- ¼ cup fresh lime juice
- 2 tablespoons kosher salt
- Black pepper to taste

Direction

- Stir together the oil, onion, garlic and cumin in a 5-quart dish with a tightly fitted lid. Cook, uncovered, at 100 percent power in a 650- to 700-watt oven for 7 minutes.
- Stir in eggplant. Cook, covered, for 5 minutes.
- Stir in bell pepper and jalapeno. Cook, covered, for 1 minute.
- Stir in zucchini, beans, tomatoes, and reserved tomato liquid. Cook, covered, for 14 minutes, stirring once halfway through cooking.
- Stir in coriander. Cook, covered, for 2 minutes.
- Remove from oven. Uncover. Stir in lime juice, salt and pepper.

Nutrition Information

- 199: calories;
- 1 gram: saturated fat;
- 0 grams: trans fat;
- 27 grams: carbohydrates;
- 9 grams: fat;
- 6 grams: monounsaturated fat;
- 2 grams: polyunsaturated fat;
- 11 grams: dietary fiber;
- 7 grams: protein;
- 664 milligrams: sodium;

19. Black Bean And Goat Cheese Quesadillas

Serving: One serving | Prep: | Cook: | Ready in: 5mins

Ingredients

- 2 corn tortillas
- ⅓ cup cooked black beans
- 1 ounce crumbled goat cheese (1/4 cup)
- ¼ roasted red bell pepper or 1/2 roasted piquilo pepper, cut in strips
- Salsa for serving (optional)

Direction

- In a microwave: Place a corn tortilla on a plate. Top with the beans. Gently mash the beans with the back of a spoon. Top with pepper strips. Sprinkle on the cheese, and top with the remaining tortilla. Press down gently, then microwave for 1 to 1 1/2 minutes until the cheese has melted. Remove from the microwave, cut into quarters or sixths and serve.
- In a pan: Place a corn tortilla in a pan. Top with the beans. Gently mash the beans with the back of a spoon. Top with pepper strips. Sprinkle on the cheese. Turn the heat on medium-high, and heat until the cheese begins to melt and the tortilla begins to brown. Place the remaining tortilla on top of the cheese, and press down lightly. Flip the quesadilla over in the pan, and heat for about 30 seconds to a minute or until the cheese has melted. Flip back over, and remove to a plate. Cut into quarters or sixths, and serve.

Nutrition Information

- 304: calories;
- 8 grams: dietary fiber;
- 229 milligrams: sodium;
- 16 grams: protein;
- 11 grams: fat;
- 7 grams: saturated fat;
- 3 grams: monounsaturated fat;

- 1 gram: sugars;
- 36 grams: carbohydrates;

20. Blackberry Sorbet

Serving: 10 servings | Prep: | Cook: |Ready in: 18mins

Ingredients

- 2 cups sugar
- 2 cups water
- 4 cups blackberries
- 2 to 3 tablespoons fresh lemon juice
- 2 tablespoons black currant syrup

Direction

- Stir sugar and water together in a 2 1/2-quart souffle dish. Cook, uncovered, at 100 percent in a high-power oven for 3 minutes. Stir thoroughly, being sure there are no grains on the bottom of the dish. Cover with a lid or microwave plastic wrap. Cook for 6 minutes. Prick plastic, if used, to release steam.
- Remove from oven and uncover. Let cool. Refrigerate until cold, several hours or overnight.
- Pass blackberries through a food mill fitted with the fine disk. Whisk in lemon juice, black currant syrup and sugar syrup. Refrigerate until cold.
- Place in an ice-cream machine and freeze according to manufacturer's instructions.

Nutrition Information

- 191: calories;
- 0 grams: polyunsaturated fat;
- 48 grams: carbohydrates;
- 3 grams: dietary fiber;
- 45 grams: sugars;
- 1 gram: protein;
- 4 milligrams: sodium;

21. Blanc Manger

Serving: 6 servings | Prep: | Cook: |Ready in: 20mins

Ingredients

- 1 ½ cups heavy cream, chilled
- ¾ cup whole milk
- ¾ cup ground almonds
- ½ cup sugar
- 1 packet powdered gelatin
- 1 to 2 tablespoons kirsch or 2 teaspoons pure vanilla extract
- 1 cup raspberries or assorted soft ripe fruit cut in small cubes

Direction

- Fill a large bowl with ice cubes and cold water. Have ready a smaller bowl that fits into the ice-water bath.
- Whip cream until it holds soft peaks. Refrigerate.
- Bring milk, almonds and sugar to a boil over medium heat, stirring occasionally to make certain the sugar dissolves. While milk heats, put gelatin and 3 tablespoons cold water in a microwave-safe bowl or a saucepan. When the gelatin is soft and spongy — it should take about 2 minutes — heat it in a microwave oven for 15 seconds (or cook it over low heat to dissolve). Stir the gelatin into the hot milk mixture, and remove the saucepan from heat.
- Pour the hot almond milk into the small reserved bowl, and set the bowl into the ice-water bath. Stir in kirsch or vanilla, and continue to stir until the mixture is cool but still liquid; you do not want the milk to gel in the bowl.
- Very gently fold the cold whipped cream into the almond milk with a rubber spatula, then fold in the berries. Spoon the blanc-manger into an 8-inch cake pan that is 2 inches high, and refrigerate until set, about 2 hours. The blanc-manger can be covered and kept in the refrigerator for up to 24 hours.

- To unmold the blanc-manger, dip the cake pan up to its rim in hot water for 5 seconds, then wipe the pan and invert the blanc-manger onto a serving plate. Serve immediately or chill until needed. Serve raspberry coulis on the side.

Nutrition Information

- 394: calories;
- 9 grams: protein;
- 47 milligrams: sodium;
- 0 grams: trans fat;
- 29 grams: fat;
- 15 grams: saturated fat;
- 10 grams: monounsaturated fat;
- 2 grams: dietary fiber;
- 26 grams: carbohydrates;
- 21 grams: sugars;

22. Blueberry Maple Caiprissimo

Serving: Two drinks | Prep: | Cook: |Ready in: 2mins

Ingredients

- 3 ½ ounces maple syrup
- 2 rosemary sprigs, cut into short pieces
- 3 ounces Cognac
- 3 ounces blueberries
- 2 ounces lemon juice

Direction

- In a microwave-safe glass or mug, stir together the syrup and rosemary. Microwave on high for about 30 seconds. When cool, discard rosemary.
- Add rosemary-flavored syrup to remaining ingredients in a blender. Add 1 1/2 cups ice. Purée until smooth, adding more ice if needed to achieve a consistency that is no longer liquid, but still pours freely.

Nutrition Information

- 264: calories;
- 1 gram: protein;
- 0 grams: polyunsaturated fat;
- 42 grams: carbohydrates;
- 2 grams: dietary fiber;
- 35 grams: sugars;
- 8 milligrams: sodium;

23. Bolognese Sauce

Serving: 8 servings | Prep: | Cook: |Ready in: 26mins

Ingredients

- 1 small onion, peeled and cut in 1/4-inch dice
- 1 small carrot, trimmed, peeled and cut in 1/4-inch dice
- 1 small rib celery, trimmed, peeled and cut in 1/4-inch dice
- 2 ounces pancetta, cut in 1/4-inch dice
- ½ ounce dried porcini mushrooms (about 1/2 cup), rinsed and finely chopped
- ½ pound ground beef
- ½ pound ground pork
- ¼ pound ground veal
- 3 ½ cups plum tomato sauce (see Micro-Tip)
- 1 tablespoon kosher salt
- ¼ teaspoon freshly ground black pepper

Direction

- Combine onion, carrot and celery in a 2 1/2-quart souffle dish with a tightly fitting lid. Cook, covered, at 100 percent power in a high-power oven for 4 minutes.
- Remove from oven and uncover. Stir in pancetta, mushrooms and meats. Cook, covered, for 2 minutes. Uncover and stir well. Mash the mixture repeatedly with the back of a wooden spoon to break up clumps of meat. Cook again, covered, for 2 minutes. Repeat stirring and mashing. Cook, covered, for 1 minute 30 seconds.

- Remove dish from oven and uncover. Stir well and break up any remaining clumps of meat. Stir in tomato sauce. Cook, uncovered, for 5 minutes.
- Remove from oven. Stir in salt and pepper.

Nutrition Information

- 264: calories;
- 613 milligrams: sodium;
- 6 grams: saturated fat;
- 0 grams: trans fat;
- 5 grams: sugars;
- 16 grams: protein;
- 17 grams: fat;
- 7 grams: monounsaturated fat;
- 1 gram: polyunsaturated fat;
- 14 grams: carbohydrates;
- 3 grams: dietary fiber;

24. Braised Leeks With Lemons

Serving: 8 servings as a side dish | Prep: | Cook: | Ready in: 1hours

Ingredients

- 5 pounds leeks, trimmed to 6 to 7 inches from the root end and washed well
- 5 cups chicken or vegetable broth
- 2 lemons, sliced very thin and seeded
- ½ cup olive oil
- Kosher salt and freshly ground black pepper to taste

Direction

- Place leeks in 2 layers in a 14-by-9-by-2-inch oval dish. Pour broth over leeks. Place lemon slices evenly over leeks. Drizzle olive oil over lemons.
- Cover tightly with microwave plastic wrap. Cook at 100 percent power in a high-power

oven for 50 minutes. Prick plastic to release steam.
- Remove from oven and uncover. Season with salt and pepper. Serve hot or cold.

Nutrition Information

- 301: calories;
- 5 grams: protein;
- 1057 milligrams: sodium;
- 14 grams: fat;
- 2 grams: polyunsaturated fat;
- 6 grams: dietary fiber;
- 12 grams: sugars;
- 10 grams: monounsaturated fat;
- 43 grams: carbohydrates;

25. Braised Potatoes And Carrots

Serving: Four servings | Prep: | Cook: | Ready in: 15mins

Ingredients

- 1 pound potatoes, peeled and cut into 1-inch pieces
- 12 ounces carrots, peeled and cut into 1-inch pieces
- ½ cup chicken broth, canned or homemade

Direction

- Combine all the ingredients in a half-quart souffle dish. Cover tightly with microwave plastic wrap and cook at 100 percent power in a 650- to 700-watt microwave oven for 10 minutes. Prick the plastic to release steam.
- Remove from the oven and uncover. Add to the roast chicken.

Nutrition Information

- 133: calories;
- 108 milligrams: sodium;
- 1 gram: fat;

- 0 grams: polyunsaturated fat;
- 29 grams: carbohydrates;
- 5 grams: sugars;
- 4 grams: protein;

26. Bread Crumbs

Serving: 1 1/2 cups | Prep: | Cook: | Ready in: 11mins

Ingredients

- 1 1-pound loaf white bread, crusts removed

Direction

- Crumble bread in food processor. Spread in a thin layer in a 10-inch round dish. Cook at 100 percent power for 8 minutes, stirring twice.
- Remove from oven and cool. For very fine crumbs, process again.

Nutrition Information

- 202: calories;
- 1 gram: polyunsaturated fat;
- 384 milligrams: sodium;
- 2 grams: fat;
- 0 grams: monounsaturated fat;
- 37 grams: carbohydrates;
- 3 grams: dietary fiber;
- 4 grams: sugars;
- 8 grams: protein;

27. Breakfast Wheat Berries

Serving: Serves 4 to 6 | Prep: | Cook: | Ready in: 1hours30mins

Ingredients

- 1 cup wheat berries
- 5 cups water
- Salt to taste
- ¼ cup honey, agave syrup or brown sugar, or more to taste
- ½ to 1 teaspoon rose water, to taste
- 1 teaspoon ground anise or fennel seeds
- ¾ teaspoon ground cinnamon
- ⅛ teaspoon freshly grated nutmeg
- ½ cup raisins or other chopped dried fruit of choice
- ⅓ cup chopped walnuts, almonds, hazelnuts, or a mixture for garnish
- 2 cups plain low-fat yogurt (optional)
- Pomegranate seeds for garnish (optional)

Direction

- The night before, combine wheat berries, 1 quart of the water and salt and bring to a boil in a saucepan. Reduce heat, cover and simmer 1 hour. Remove from heat, stir in the honey, agave syrup or sugar, rose water, anise or fennel seeds, cinnamon, nutmeg and raisins or dried fruit. Cover and leave overnight (or for 5 to 6 hours).
- In the morning, add remaining cup of water to the wheat berries and bring to a simmer. Cook 30 to 45 minutes, stirring often, until berries are soft and splayed at one end. There should be some liquid surrounding the wheat berries (add more water if necessary). Taste and add more sweetener if desired.
- Serve on their own with some of the liquid in the saucepan (stir in some milk if desired), or spoon about 1/3 cup yogurt into bowls and top with a generous spoonful of the berries, with some of the sweet broth. Top with a handful of chopped nuts and a few pomegranate seeds if desired.

Nutrition Information

- 170: calories;
- 5 grams: dietary fiber;
- 17 grams: sugars;
- 3 grams: protein;
- 591 milligrams: sodium;
- 1 gram: fat;

- 0 grams: polyunsaturated fat;
- 41 grams: carbohydrates;

28. Broccoli Baked In Cheese Sauce

Serving: 6 to 8 servings | Prep: | Cook: | Ready in: 35mins

Ingredients

- 5 tablespoons cornstarch
- 2 teaspoons curry powder
- 1 teaspoon kosher salt
- 2 cups skim milk
- 3 dashes hot red-pepper sauce
- 1 ¼ cups grated part-skim mozzarella (about 5 3/4 ounces)
- 1 pound cooked broccoli florets and stems (see Micro Tip)

Direction

- Mix cornstarch, curry powder and salt in a 2 1/2-quart souffle dish. Pour in a little of the milk and stir until cornstarch is completely dissolved. Stir in remaining milk. Cover tightly with lid or microwave plastic wrap. Cook at 100 percent power in a 650- to 700-watt oven for 4 minutes. Prick plastic to release steam.
- Remove from oven and uncover. Scrape corners and bottom of dish with a wooden spoon. Whisk well to dissolve any lumps. Cover, return to oven and cook for 3 minutes. Prick plastic to release steam.
- Remove from oven and uncover. Whisk in red pepper sauce and 1 cup of the cheese.
- Scrape sauce into a large bowl. Stir in broccoli. Put mixture in an oval dish, 13 by 9 by 2 inches. Cook, covered with plastic, for 5 minutes. Prick plastic to release steam. Uncover and stir. Re-cover and cook for 7 minutes. Prick plastic. While broccoli is cooking, preheat broiler.

- Remove dish from oven and uncover. Sprinkle with remaining cheese. Run a small knife around the inside edge of the dish to prevent sticking. Put dish under broiler until cheese browns, about 6 minutes. Remove from oven and serve warm.

Nutrition Information

- 119: calories;
- 5 grams: fat;
- 3 grams: sugars;
- 1 gram: monounsaturated fat;
- 0 grams: dietary fiber;
- 11 grams: carbohydrates;
- 8 grams: protein;
- 336 milligrams: sodium;

29. Broccoli Rabe With Italian Sausage

Serving: Four servings as a main course | Prep: | Cook: | Ready in: 30mins

Ingredients

- 1 ½ pounds hot or sweet Italian sausage, cut across into 1-inch thick pieces
- 1 pound broccoli rabe, trimmed and cut across into 1-inch pieces
- 4 ½ tablespoons olive oil
- ¾ teaspoon crushed red-pepper flakes, if using sweet sausage
- ¾ teaspoon kosher salt
- Freshly ground black pepper to taste

Direction

- Place the sausage in a 9-inch pie plate, and cover with a paper towel. Cook at 100 percent power in a high-power oven for 11 minutes. Remove from oven and uncover. Pour off liquid and set aside.

- Place the broccoli rabe in a 14-by-9-by-2-inch oval dish. Toss with the olive oil and red-pepper flakes, if using. Cover tightly with microwave plastic wrap. Cook for 8 minutes. Prick plastic to release steam.
- Remove from oven and uncover. Stir in salt, pepper and cooked sausage. Serve alone or over cooked pasta.

Nutrition Information

- 415: calories;
- 8 grams: saturated fat;
- 17 grams: monounsaturated fat;
- 3 grams: dietary fiber;
- 0 grams: sugars;
- 31 grams: protein;
- 1008 milligrams: sodium;
- 30 grams: fat;
- 7 grams: carbohydrates;

30. Broccoli Spears In Indian Spice Dressing

Serving: 6 to 8 servings | Prep: | Cook: | Ready in: 1hours35mins

Ingredients

- 2 tablespoons amchoor (mango powder)
- 1 cup water
- 2 tablespoons sesame seeds
- 1 ½ teaspoons black mustard seeds
- ¼ teaspoon hulled cardamom seeds
- 3 tablespoons dark sesame oil
- 4 large cloves garlic, peeled and chopped coarse
- Pinch red pepper flakes
- 1 tablespoon kosher salt
- 2 pounds cooked broccoli spears with florets (see Micro Tip)

Direction

- Combine amchoor and water in a 1- to 1 1/2-quart souffle dish. Cover tightly with microwave plastic wrap. Cook at 100 percent power in a 650- to 700-watt oven for 5 minutes. Prick plastic to release steam. Remove from oven. Uncover and reserve.
- Put sesame seeds in a 1-quart souffle dish. Cook, uncovered, for 4 minutes. Stir in mustard seeds. Cook, uncovered, for 2 minutes. Stir in cardamom seeds and sesame oil. Cook, uncovered, for 2 minutes. Stir in garlic and red pepper flakes. Cook, uncovered, for 2 minutes.
- Remove from oven. Stir reserved amchoor liquid into seed mixture. Stir in salt. Allow to cool.
- Seeds from dressing will rise to the top; spoon them over the broccoli florets. Pour remaining dressing over all. Let broccoli marinate 1 to 2 hours at room temperature (or longer in the refrigerator), occasionally spooning dressing over the spears.

Nutrition Information

- 104: calories;
- 9 grams: carbohydrates;
- 2 grams: sugars;
- 4 grams: protein;
- 363 milligrams: sodium;
- 7 grams: fat;
- 1 gram: saturated fat;
- 3 grams: dietary fiber;

31. Broccoli And Red Onion Quesadillas

Serving: Two quesadillas | Prep: | Cook: | Ready in: 10mins

Ingredients

- 1 large broccoli crown, about 1/2 pound
- 1 tablespoon extra virgin olive oil

- 1 medium red onion, cut in half lengthwise, then sliced across the grain
- 1 tablespoon chopped cilantro or epazote (optional)
- Salt
- freshly ground pepper
- 4 corn tortillas
- 2 ounces grated Monterey Jack, Cheddar or mixed cheeses (1/2 cup)
- Salsa for serving (optional)

Direction

- Make the broccoli filling. Steam the broccoli crown for four minutes, then remove from the heat. Rinse with cold water and pat dry. Slice 1/4 inch thick. Heat the oil over medium-high heat in a large, heavy frying pan, and add the red onion. Cook, stirring, until tender and seared on the edges. Add the sliced broccoli. Cook, stirring, until seared on the edges, about three minutes. Stir in the cilantro or epazote, season with salt and pepper, and remove from the heat. Taste and adjust seasoning.
- In a microwave: Place a corn tortilla on a plate. Top with half the broccoli and onions, and spread in an even layer. Sprinkle on half the cheese, and top with another tortilla. Press down gently, then microwave for 1 to 1 1/2 minutes until the cheese has melted. Remove from the microwave, cut into quarters or sixths, and serve. Repeat with the remaining ingredients.
- In a pan: Place a corn tortilla in a pan. Top with half the broccoli and onions, and spread in an even layer. Sprinkle on half the cheese. Turn the heat on medium-high, and heat until the cheese begins to melt and the tortilla begins to brown. Place another tortilla on top of the cheese, and press down lightly. Flip over the quesadilla in the pan, and heat for about 30 seconds or until the cheese has melted. Flip back over, and remove to a plate. Cut into quarters or sixths, and serve. Repeat with the remaining ingredients.

Nutrition Information

- 343: calories;
- 2 grams: polyunsaturated fat;
- 34 grams: carbohydrates;
- 7 grams: dietary fiber;
- 14 grams: protein;
- 19 grams: fat;
- 8 grams: monounsaturated fat;
- 5 grams: sugars;
- 553 milligrams: sodium;

32. Brown Sugar Caramels

Serving: 100 squares | Prep: | Cook: |Ready in: 25mins

Ingredients

- Vegetable oil for coating pan
- 1 cup heavy cream
- ½ cup milk
- ¾ cup granulated sugar
- ¾ cup dark brown sugar
- 2 tablespoons unsalted butter

Direction

- Oil an 8-by-8-by-2-inch square pan. Cut a piece of wax paper to fit bottom of pan; oil. Place paper in pan and reserve.
- Combine cream and milk in a 2-quart souffle dish. Cover tightly with microwave plastic wrap. Cook at 100 percent power in a high-power microwave oven for 3 minutes. Prick plastic to release steam.
- Remove from oven and uncover. Stir in sugars until dissolved. Cook, uncovered, for 18 minutes, stirring carefully twice.
- Remove from oven and stir in butter until melted. Pour into the reserved pan, scraping thoroughly.
- Refrigerate until set firm, several hours or overnight. Run the tip of a small knife around inside edge of pan. Use the knife to lift the caramel and paper out of the pan. Cut into

small squares. Peel the paper away from the caramels. Wrap and store in refrigerator

Nutrition Information

- 22: calories;
- 0 grams: protein;
- 3 grams: sugars;
- 2 milligrams: sodium;
- 1 gram: saturated fat;

33. Carrot And Ginger Terrine

Serving: 4 servings | Prep: | Cook: | Ready in: 4hours20mins

Ingredients

- 1 pound carrots, trimmed, peeled and cut in 1/4-inch rounds
- ½ teaspoon turmeric
- ¼ cup water
- 1 ½ envelopes unflavored gelatin
- ¼ cup plus 2 tablespoons chicken broth
- ¼ cup fromage blanc
- 2 ¼ teaspoons grated, peeled fresh ginger
- Kosher salt to taste
- Freshly ground black pepper
- 1 scallion, sliced thin
- Spinach and coriander sauce (see recipe)

Direction

- Toss carrots with turmeric in a 13-by-9-by-2-inch oval dish. Cover tightly with microwave plastic wrap. Cook at 100 percent power in a high-power oven for 8 minutes. Prick plastic to release steam.
- Remove from oven and uncover. Transfer to a food processor and process until smooth.
- Place water in a glass 1-cup measure. Sprinkle gelatin over water. Let stand for 2 minutes. Stir. Cover with plastic wrap. Cook for 30 seconds. Prick plastic to release steam.

- Remove from oven and uncover. Pour into food processor with carrots. Add broth, fromage blanc, ginger, salt and pepper. Process until completely smooth. Taste and adjust seasonings, if needed.
- Transfer mixture to a bowl and stir in scallion. Rinse a 2- to 3-cup mold with ice water. Do not dry. Scrape mixture into mold. Cover with plastic wrap and refrigerate for at least 4 hours.
- Unmold terrine and cut into slices. Spoon spinach and coriander sauce onto four plates. Place terrine slices over sauce and serve.

Nutrition Information

- 86: calories;
- 1 gram: saturated fat;
- 14 grams: carbohydrates;
- 410 milligrams: sodium;
- 2 grams: fat;
- 0 grams: polyunsaturated fat;
- 4 grams: dietary fiber;
- 6 grams: sugars;
- 5 grams: protein;

34. Cazuela De Elsa

Serving: 4 to 6 servings | Prep: | Cook: | Ready in: 42mins

Ingredients

- ½ pound carrots (about 2 small), trimmed, scraped, halved lengthwise and cut into 2-inch lengths
- ¼ pound yellow onions (1 medium-size), peeled and cut into 1-inch wedges
- ½ pound sweet potatoes (2 small), peeled and sliced 1/4-inch thick
- 1 chicken, 2 1/2 pounds, cut into serving pieces
- 6 cloves garlic, peeled and smashed
- 1 tablespoon kosher salt

- 2 ½ cups water
- ⅓ pound tomatoes (2 medium-size), cored and cut into 2-inch cubes
- 1 large green bell pepper, stemmed, seeded, deribbed and cut into 2-inch pieces
- 2 ears fresh corn, shucked and cut across into 2-inch-wide rounds
- ¼ cup (packed) fresh coriander leaves, minced
- Freshly ground black pepper

Direction

- In a glass or ceramic dish (14 by 11 by 2 inches), combine carrots, onions and sweet potatoes. Cover tightly with microwave plastic wrap. Cook at 100 percent 5 minutes.
- Uncover carefully. Add chicken, garlic, salt and water. Arrange chicken pieces so they do not touch. Cover tightly with microwave plastic wrap. Cook at 100 percent 10 minutes.
- Uncover carefully and stir, pushing chicken pieces from center of dish toward the outside, and pieces from the outside toward the center. Turn each piece over.
- Scatter tomatoes, green pepper, corn and coriander over chicken. Cover tightly and cook at 100 percent 7 minutes. Uncover and season to taste with peppe

Nutrition Information

- 379: calories;
- 27 grams: protein;
- 1091 milligrams: sodium;
- 20 grams: fat;
- 0 grams: trans fat;
- 8 grams: sugars;
- 4 grams: dietary fiber;
- 24 grams: carbohydrates;
- 6 grams: saturated fat;

35. Celery Root Salad

Serving: 4 servings | Prep: | Cook: | Ready in: 20mins

Ingredients

- ¾ pound celery root, peeled and julienned
- ¼ cup water
- 3 tablespoons Dijon mustard
- 1 tablespoon red wine vinegar
- 3 tablespoons olive oil
- 2 teaspoons chopped flat-leaf parsley
- ¼ teaspoon kosher salt
- Freshly ground black pepper to taste

Direction

- Place celery root in a 2 1/2-quart souffle dish with a lid. Add water and cover. Holding the lid down with your thumbs, shake the dish to distribute the water evenly. Cook, covered, at 100 percent power in a high-power microwave oven for 8 minutes. Strain celery root and run under cold water until vegetables are cool.
- Put mustard in a bowl and whisk in vinegar. Gradually whisk in oil, beginning with drops and increasing to a steady stream. Add parsley and season with salt and pepper. Whisk again and toss in celery root.

Nutrition Information

- 134: calories;
- 0 grams: trans fat;
- 8 grams: monounsaturated fat;
- 9 grams: carbohydrates;
- 2 grams: protein;
- 293 milligrams: sodium;
- 11 grams: fat;
- 1 gram: sugars;

36. Celery Root Puree

Serving: Six to eight servings | Prep: | Cook: | Ready in: 30mins

Ingredients

- 3 medium celery roots (each weighing about 1 pound), peeled and cubed into about 1/2-inch squares
- 2 tablespoons unsalted butter
- 3 tablespoons heavy cream
- Salt to taste

Direction

- Place the celery root in a baking dish, dot with the butter and cover. Microwave at high - stirring once -until the celery root is soft and gives no resistance when pierced with a fork, about 20 to 25 minutes.
- Transfer the celery root to the bowl of a food processor. Add the cream and process until smooth. Taste for seasoning. (This can be prepared ahead earlier in the day and reheated.)

Nutrition Information

- 69: calories;
- 5 grams: fat;
- 3 grams: saturated fat;
- 0 grams: polyunsaturated fat;
- 1 gram: protein;
- 6 grams: carbohydrates;
- 157 milligrams: sodium;

37. Chicken In Red Wine

Serving: 8 servings (231 calories per serving) | Prep: | Cook: | Ready in: 47mins

Ingredients

- 1 teaspoon olive oil
- ½ pound mushrooms, cleaned and sliced with stems attached
- ½ pound pearl onions, peeled
- 2 chickens (2 1/2 pounds each), cut into serving pieces and skinned
- ¼ cup brandy

- 2 tablespoons red-wine vinegar
- 3 tablespoons tomato paste
- ½ teaspoon dried thyme
- 1 ½ bay leaves
- 2 teaspoons kosher salt
- 16 large garlic cloves, smashed and peeled
- 1 cup chicken broth
- 2 cups dry red wine
- ⅓ cup cornstarch
- Freshly ground black pepper to taste

Direction

- Place olive oil in the bottom of a dish 14 by 11 by 2 inches. Add mushrooms to oil and toss, making sure they are coated with oil; mound them in center of the dish. Place onions around inside edge of dish. Fit chicken breasts, meaty side up, in center of dish on top of mushrooms. Arrange the rest of the chicken around the breasts.
- Add brandy, vinegar, tomato paste, thyme, bay leaves and salt. Tuck garlic between chicken pieces. Pour broth and wine over all. Cover tightly with microwave plastic wrap. Cook at 100 percent for 22 minutes.
- Remove from oven. Prick plastic and uncover carefully. Remove chicken pieces to a serving platter and keep warm.
- Stir 1/2 cup of the cooking liquid into the cornstarch. Whisk into liquid in dish. Add pepper. Cook, uncovered, at 100 percent power for 5 minutes.
- Remove from oven. Stir well. Add chicken to sauce. Remove bay leaves. Serve immediately.

Nutrition Information

- 557: calories;
- 9 grams: saturated fat;
- 0 grams: trans fat;
- 6 grams: polyunsaturated fat;
- 16 grams: carbohydrates;
- 39 grams: protein;
- 703 milligrams: sodium;
- 30 grams: fat;

- 13 grams: monounsaturated fat;
- 2 grams: dietary fiber;
- 3 grams: sugars;

---

38. Chicken Liver Crostini

Serving: 6 servings | Prep: | Cook: | Ready in: 15mins

Ingredients

- 12 1/4-inch-thick slices Italian or French bread
- ¼ cup olive oil plus additional oil for crostini
- ¼ cup loosely packed parsley or sage leaves
- ½ pound chicken livers, cleaned
- 2 small cloves garlic, smashed, peeled and coarsely chopped
- 5 anchovy fillets in oil, rinsed
- Kosher salt and freshly ground black pepper to taste
- 1 teaspoon Hollands gin (strongly juniper-scented), optional

Direction

- Preheat the oven to 350 degrees. Place the bread slices on a baking sheet, and lightly brush top of each with some of the olive oil. Bake until the edges are a light brown and the centers are crisp, about 10 minutes.
- While the crostini bake, place the parsley in a food processor, and process until finely chopped. Transfer to a small bowl, and set aside.
- Place the livers, 1/4 cup olive oil and garlic in a 2 1/2-quart casserole with a tight-fitting lid. Cook, covered, at 100 percent power in a high-power microwave oven for 2 minutes. Stir well, re-cover, and cook for 1 minute.
- Remove from the oven and uncover. Scrape the mixture into a food processor. Add the anchovies, and process until smooth. Taste, and add salt, pepper and gin.
- Spread 1 rounded tablespoon of the chicken-liver mixture on each of the crostini. Sprinkle the tops with the reserved parsley or sage.

Nutrition Information

- 113: calories;
- 10 grams: protein;
- 280 milligrams: sodium;
- 3 grams: fat;
- 1 gram: sugars;
- 0 grams: trans fat;
- 12 grams: carbohydrates;

---

39. Chicken Soup

Serving: 8 servings | Prep: | Cook: | Ready in: 1hours30mins

Ingredients

- 4 pounds chicken bones, cut in 2-inch pieces
- 2 small carrots, peeled and cut in chunks
- 1 small onion, peeled and cut in chunks
- 1 small turnip, peeled and cut in chunks
- 1 rib celery, cut in chunks
- 1 leek, trimmed, washed and cut in chunks
- ½ small parsnip, peeled and cut in chunks
- 1 clove garlic, smashed and peeled
- Stems from 1 bunch parsley (about 1 ounce)
- 8 cups water
- ½ cup loosely packed dill sprigs, chopped
- 2 teaspoons kosher salt

Direction

- Place all ingredients except dill and salt in a 5-quart casserole with a tightly fitting lid. Cook, covered, at 100 percent power in a high-power oven for 40 minutes.
- Remove from oven and uncover. Strain through a fine sieve.
- Add dill and salt before serving. This soup can be used to poach matzoh balls or for matzoh ball soup.

Nutrition Information

- 289: calories;
- 16 grams: fat;
- 0 grams: polyunsaturated fat;
- 2 grams: sugars;
- 26 grams: protein;
- 832 milligrams: sodium;
- 6 grams: carbohydrates;
- 1 gram: dietary fiber;
- 7 grams: saturated fat;

40. Chicken With Rhubarb And Spring Vegetables

Serving: 4 servings | Prep: | Cook: | Ready in: 30mins

Ingredients

- 1 ¼ pounds rhubarb, trimmed and cut on the diagonal in 1/8-inch slices (3 cups)
- 2 pounds boneless, skinless chicken breasts (8 half-breasts)
- 1 teaspoon kosher salt
- 1 ¼ pounds asparagus, cut in 2-inch lengths using only the tip and a second piece from the tip end (save remainder for another use)
- 6 ounces red radishes, trimmed and sliced thin (1 cup)
- 4 ounces shallots (about 6), peeled and halved if small, quartered if large (1/4 cup)
- 1 ½ cups heavy cream
- 3 tablespoons cornstarch
- 3 tablespoons water
- 6 scallions, green part only, sliced thin (1/2 cup)
- Freshly ground black pepper to taste

Direction

- Place rhubarb in an even layer in a 14-by-11-by-2-inch oval dish. Arrange chicken over the rhubarb so that the thick side of the chicken is toward the inside rim of the dish. Sprinkle salt over chicken. Evenly scatter asparagus, radishes and shallots over chicken. Lightly press layers down into the dish. Pour cream over all.
- Cover tightly with microwave plastic wrap. Cook at 100 percent power in a high-power oven for 10 minutes. While dish is cooking, stir cornstarch and water until smooth.
- Prick plastic to release steam. Remove from oven and uncover. Spread scallions and pour cornstarch mixture over vegetables. Use a spoon to mix them into the cream as well as possible without disturbing the chicken. Re-cover and cook for 5 minutes. Prick plastic to release steam.
- Remove from oven and uncover. Mix in pepper and serve.

Nutrition Information

- 841: calories;
- 43 grams: fat;
- 0 grams: trans fat;
- 12 grams: monounsaturated fat;
- 22 grams: carbohydrates;
- 6 grams: dietary fiber;
- 8 grams: sugars;
- 90 grams: protein;
- 687 milligrams: sodium;
- 23 grams: saturated fat;
- 3 grams: polyunsaturated fat;

41. Chicken And Ham Terrine

Serving: 8 one-inch slices | Prep: | Cook: | Ready in: 10mins

Ingredients

- 2 cups fresh bread crumbs from about 6 slices white bread
- ½ cup chicken broth
- ½ cup chopped fresh parsley
- 1 ½ teaspoons dried sage
- ⅛ teaspoon cayenne pepper

- Freshly ground black pepper
- 3 skinless, boneless chicken breast halves, cut into 1-inch pieces
- 12 ounces baked ham, rind removed, cut into 1-inch pieces
- 3 shallots, peeled and quartered

Direction

- Place bread crumbs, chicken broth, parsley, sage, cayenne and black pepper in a medium-size bowl and mix well. Reserve.
- Place chicken, ham and shallots in bowl of food processor. Process until finely chopped. Add reserved bread-crumb mixture and puree.
- Scrape mixture into a glass or ceramic loaf pan, 9 by 5 by 3 inches, that either has a nonstick surface or has been sprayed with nonstick vegetable spray. Smooth out surface with spatula. Cover pan tightly with microwave plastic wrap. Cook at 100 percent power in a 650- to 700- watt oven for 5 minutes. Prick plastic to release steam.
- Remove from oven and uncover. Cover lightly with kitchen towel and allow to stand for 10 minutes. Invert onto serving plate.

Nutrition Information

- 323: calories;
- 0 grams: trans fat;
- 1 gram: polyunsaturated fat;
- 26 grams: carbohydrates;
- 2 grams: saturated fat;
- 4 grams: sugars;
- 35 grams: protein;
- 756 milligrams: sodium;
- 8 grams: fat;
- 3 grams: dietary fiber;

42. Chickpea Casserole

Serving: 4 servings | Prep: | Cook: | Ready in: 35mins

Ingredients

- ½ pound eggplant, cut into 3/4-inch pieces
- 2 tablespoons toasted sesame oil
- ¼ cup wheat germ
- ¾ cup tomato puree
- ¼ cup soy sauce
- 6 medium cloves garlic, sliced in quarters lengthwise
- 1 medium onion, peeled, cut in half and sliced
- ¼ pound mushrooms, wiped clean with a damp cloth, stems trimmed flush to caps and sliced thin across caps
- 3 cups canned chickpeas, washed and drained; or cooked chickpeas (see Microtip)
- 8 cups spinach cut across the stem into thin slices, or 2 boxes frozen spinach defrosted under warm running water
- ½ teaspoon red pepper flakes
- 5 ounces frozen peas, thawed
- Freshly ground black pepper to taste
- 1 ½ tablespoons sesame seeds
- ½ pound smoked mozzarella, sliced thin

Direction

- Toss eggplant and oil in a 5-quart casserole with a lid. Cover and cook at 100 percent power in a high-power microwave oven for 6 minutes.
- Stir in wheat germ, tomato puree, soy sauce, garlic, onion, mushrooms and chickpeas. Place spinach on top (or if using defrosted, stir in) and sprinkle with red pepper flakes. Cook, covered, for 8 minutes.
- Pour peas in and grind black pepper into casserole. Mix, being sure to break up any clump of spinach. Sprinkle with sesame seeds and place cheese in one layer on top. Cook, uncovered, 4 minutes, or until cheese is melted. Serve immediately.

Nutrition Information

- 583: calories;
- 6 grams: polyunsaturated fat;
- 14 grams: sugars;

- 34 grams: protein;
- 1706 milligrams: sodium;
- 26 grams: fat;
- 9 grams: saturated fat;
- 8 grams: monounsaturated fat;
- 60 grams: carbohydrates;
- 18 grams: dietary fiber;

43. Chilean Stuffed Grape Leaves

Serving: 45 to 50 stuffed leaves | Prep: | Cook: |Ready in: 1hours30mins

Ingredients

- 1 jar grape leaves in brine, or 45 to 50 fresh leaves soaked in brine
- 1 tablespoon olive oil
- ⅓ cup finely chopped onion
- 1 small clove garlic, peeled, smashed and chopped fine
- ½ teaspoon ground cumin
- 6 tablespoons long-grain rice
- 3 ½ cups beef broth
- 6 ounces lean ground beef
- 4 teaspoons finely chopped parsley
- 1 ½ teaspoons kosher salt
- Freshly ground black pepper to taste

Direction

- Drain grape leaves and rinse well under cold running water. Allow to soak in fresh water for at least 1 hour.
- Place olive oil in 1-quart souffle dish. Cook, uncovered, at 100 percent power in a high-power oven for 1 1/2 minutes. Stir in onion, garlic and cumin. Cook, uncovered, for 1 1/2 minutes.
- Stir in rice and 3/4 cup of the broth. Cover tightly with microwave plastic wrap. Cook for 10 minutes. Prick plastic to release steam.
- Remove from oven and uncover. Allow to cool slightly. Stir in beef, parsley, salt and pepper.

- Place one grape leaf outside down on work surface. Remove stem with a small knife. Place 1 rounded teaspoon of the rice mixture in the center of the leaf. Fold the sides to the center and roll up. Place, seam side down in an 11-by- 7 by 2 1/2-inch glass dish. Repeat with remaining rice mixture and leaves.
- Pour 1 1/2 cups of the broth over the grape leaves. Cook, covered, for 18 minutes. Prick plastic to release steam.
- Remove from oven and uncover. Allow to stand until cool. Pour over remaining 1 1/4 cups beef broth. Cover and refrigerate for at least 2 hours.

Nutrition Information

- 30: calories;
- 1 gram: sugars;
- 0 grams: polyunsaturated fat;
- 3 grams: carbohydrates;
- 2 grams: protein;
- 80 milligrams: sodium;

44. Chili Pate

Serving: 1 8-by-4-inch loaf; makes 28 slices or 112 canapes | Prep: | Cook: |Ready in: 12hours25mins

Ingredients

- 1 tablespoon vegetable oil
- 2 ¼ teaspoons cumin
- ½ teaspoon red pepper flakes
- 1 ½ pounds very lean ground round of beef
- ¼ pound kidney fat, coarsely chopped
- 3 large cloves garlic, peeled and crushed
- 1 small onion, coarsely chopped
- 2 teaspoons kosher salt
- Freshly ground black pepper to taste
- ½ cup loosely packed coriander (cilantro) leaves
- 1 35-ounce can plum tomatoes, squeezed and drained thoroughly

- 1 cup canned red beans, drained and rinsed, or home-prepared beans

Direction

- Stir oil, cumin and red pepper together in a 1-cup glass measure. Cook at 100 percent power in a high-power oven (see Micro Tip) for 1 minute 30 seconds. Remove from oven and set aside.
- Place ground round, fat, garlic, onion, salt, pepper and reserved oil-spice mixture in a food processor. Process until onion is finely chopped. Add coriander and tomatoes and process until coriander is coarsely chopped. Scrape mixture into a bowl and stir in beans.
- Place mixture in a loaf pan, 9 by 5 by 3 inches. Cover with microwave plastic wrap. Cook for 12 minutes. Pierce plastic to release steam.
- Remove from oven and uncover. Cover with a towel for 10 minutes. Uncover and let stand until cool. Wrap pan tightly with foil or plastic wrap and place weight on the pate. Refrigerate for 8 to 12 hours. Uncover and unmold onto a plate. Cut into 1/4-inch slices.

Nutrition Information

- 73: calories;
- 2 grams: fat;
- 1 gram: sugars;
- 0 grams: polyunsaturated fat;
- 7 grams: protein;
- 3 grams: dietary fiber;
- 158 milligrams: sodium;

45. Chilled Curried Pea Soup

Serving: Four servings | Prep: | Cook: | Ready in: 1hours20mins

Ingredients

- 1 medium onion, peeled and coarsely chopped, about 1 cup

- 1 ½ tablespoons curry powder
- 1 tablespoon vegetable oil
- 1 ¼ pounds fresh shelled peas or 2 10-ounce packages frozen peas, thawed
- 3 cups meat broth (see recipe)
- ½ cup plain low-fat yogurt
- 2 teaspoons fresh lime juice
- Kosher salt and freshly ground pepper to taste

Direction

- Combine the onion, curry powder and oil in a two-and-one-half-quart souffle dish or casserole with a tightly fitting lid. Cover and cook at 100 percent power in a 650- to 700-watt oven for three minutes.
- Remove and uncover. Stir in the peas and broth. Cover and cook at 100 percent power for five minutes.
- Remove and uncover. Pass through a food mill fitted with a fine blade to remove the skins. Discard the pulp, transfer the soup to a blender or food processor and puree until smooth. Return the soup to the souffle dish and refrigerate at least an hour, until chilled.
- Just before serving, stir in the yogurt and lime juice. Season with salt and pepper.

Nutrition Information

- 183: calories;
- 5 grams: fat;
- 0 grams: trans fat;
- 3 grams: monounsaturated fat;
- 27 grams: carbohydrates;
- 11 grams: sugars;
- 10 grams: protein;
- 1 gram: polyunsaturated fat;
- 8 grams: dietary fiber;
- 883 milligrams: sodium;

46. Chilled Fennel Soup

Serving: 8 cups | Prep: | Cook: | Ready in: 45mins

Ingredients

- 5 pounds fennel (5 medium bulbs), trimmed of tops and root ends (reserve tops for garnish) and cut in 1-inch cubes
- 3 tablespoons olive oil
- 8 ounces fromage blanc, or skim milk or low-fat cottage cheese
- 2 tablespoons fresh lemon juice
- 4 cups chicken broth
- 1 tablespoon kosher salt
- Freshly ground pepper to taste

Direction

- Place fennel in a 5-quart casserole with a tightly fitting lid. Toss with olive oil. Cook, covered, at 100 percent power in a high-power microwave oven for 32 minutes, stirring twice.
- Remove from oven and uncover. Immediately scrape mixture into a food processor. Process for several minutes, stopping from time to time to scrape sides of bowl, until mixture is very smooth.
- Add fromage blanc and process until smooth. Add lemon juice and 2 cups of the chicken broth and process until smooth.
- Scrape mixture into a large bowl. Whisk in remaining 2 cups chicken broth, salt and pepper.
- Refrigerate until cold. Coarsely chop 1/2 cup of the fennel tops and sprinkle some over each serving.

Nutrition Information

- 153: calories;
- 11 grams: fat;
- 3 grams: saturated fat;
- 6 grams: monounsaturated fat;
- 7 grams: protein;
- 488 milligrams: sodium;
- 1 gram: polyunsaturated fat;
- 8 grams: carbohydrates;
- 0 grams: dietary fiber;
- 4 grams: sugars;

47. Chinese Bass

Serving: 3 to 4 servings | Prep: | Cook: | Ready in: 16mins

Ingredients

- 2 pounds whole black bass, cleaned and gutted with head on
- 2 cloves garlic, smashed, peeled and halved
- 3 slices fresh ginger, about the size of a quarter, peeled and julienned
- 1 tablespoon dried Chinese black beans
- 2 sprigs coriander
- 3 tablespoons Tamari soy sauce
- 1 tablespoon sesame oil
- 1 tablespoon rice vinegar
- 2 scallions, cleaned; green and white parts cut into 2-inch lengths

Direction

- Slash across the fish twice, on the diagonal, on each side. Place fish on an oval platter 14 by 8 inches.
- Place garlic on platter around fish. Scatter remaining ingredients over fish. Cover tightly with polyvinyl plastic (PV) wrap.
- Place platter in microwave oven. Cook at 100 percent power (high setting) 11 minutes. Remove from oven. Uncover and serve hot.

Nutrition Information

- 292: calories;
- 10 grams: fat;
- 2 grams: saturated fat;
- 7 grams: carbohydrates;
- 43 grams: protein;
- 3 grams: dietary fiber;
- 1 gram: sugars;
- 914 milligrams: sodium;
- 4 grams: monounsaturated fat;

48. Chinese Chicken And Vegetables

Serving: 4 servings | Prep: | Cook: | Ready in: 20mins

Ingredients

- 2 medium yellow or red bell peppers (7 ounces each), cored, ribbed and cut in strips 1/4-inch thick
- 3 tablespoons black soy sauce
- 2 tablespoons rice-wine vinegar
- 1 tablespoon grated, peeled fresh ginger
- 2 ½ teaspoons Chinese chili paste with garlic
- 2 teaspoons toasted sesame oil
- 2 medium zucchini (5 ounces each), trimmed, halved crosswise and cut in strips 1/4-inch thick
- 1 ¼ pounds boneless, skinless chicken breasts (5 half-breasts), cut on the diagonal in strips 1/2-inch thick
- 2 tablespoons cornstarch
- 2 tablespoons water
- 2 tablespoons scallions, green part only, sliced thin

Direction

- Place peppers in a 13-by-9-by-2-inch oval dish. Cover tightly with microwave plastic wrap. Cook at 100 percent power in a high-power oven for 2 minutes, 30 seconds. Prick plastic to release steam.
- While peppers are cooking, stir together soy, vinegar, ginger, chili paste and sesame oil.
- Remove dish from oven and uncover. Stir in zucchini. Place chicken over vegetables in an even layer. Pour soy mixture over chicken. Re-cover and cook for 3 minutes. Prick plastic to release steam.
- While chicken mixture is cooking, stir cornstarch and water together. Uncover dish. Stir in scallions and cornstarch mixture. Re-cover and cook for 2 minutes 45 seconds. Prick plastic to release steam.
- Remove from oven and uncover. Serve over cooked white rice.

Nutrition Information

- 369: calories;
- 0 grams: trans fat;
- 3 grams: dietary fiber;
- 12 grams: carbohydrates;
- 9 grams: fat;
- 2 grams: polyunsaturated fat;
- 5 grams: sugars;
- 57 grams: protein;
- 778 milligrams: sodium;

49. Chinese Pork Stuffed Cabbage

Serving: 18 cabbage rolls | Prep: | Cook: | Ready in: 30mins

Ingredients

- 2 pork chops with the bone (6 ounces each), or 1/2 pound boneless pork chops, cut in 1-inch chunks, including a small amount of the surrounding fat
- ½ cup loosely packed cilantro leaves
- 2 medium-size cloves garlic, peeled and smashed
- ½ teaspoon Chinese five-spice powder
- 2 teaspoons soy sauce
- 2 ½ tablespoons sliced water chestnuts, cut in 1/8-inch cubes
- 1 large head cabbage (2 1/2 pounds), blanched
- 2 tablespoons water

Direction

- Place pork, cilantro and garlic in a food processor and pulse until pork is ground and cilantro is coarsely chopped. Add spice powder and soy sauce and process until combined. Stir in water chestnuts.

- Carefully separate nine cabbage leaves. Cut each leaf in half, removing the center rib. Trim the heavy white sections from each half, leaving a rough 4 1/2-inch square.
- Place one cabbage leaf outside down on work surface. Drop 1 level tablespoon of the pork in the top third of the leaf. Fold the top of the leaf over the filling. Fold the sides of the leaf over the filling, then roll up as tight as possible. Repeat with remaining leaves and pork mixture.
- Arrange stuffed leaves in three rows in an 11-by-7 by 2 1/2-inch glass dish. Sprinkle with water. Cover tightly with microwave plastic wrap. Cook at 100 percent power in a high-power oven for 7 minutes. Prick plastic to release steam.
- Remove from oven and uncover.

Nutrition Information

- 55: calories;
- 1 gram: monounsaturated fat;
- 0 grams: polyunsaturated fat;
- 4 grams: carbohydrates;
- 5 grams: protein;
- 56 milligrams: sodium;
- 2 grams: sugars;

50. Chinese Stewed Tomatoes And Peppers

Serving: Six cups, about 10 servings | Prep: | Cook: | Ready in: 25mins

Ingredients

- 6 cloves garlic, smashed and peeled
- 2 scallions, both green and white parts, trimmed and cut in 2-inch pieces
- ½ cup coriander leaves and stems
- 1 tablespoon peanut oil

- 1 pound sweet-hot peppers, such as gypsy, Hungarian or poblano, cored, seeded, deribbed and cut into 3-by- 1/2-inch strips
- 2 ½ pounds ripe tomatoes, cored and cut into 1/2-inch-wide wedges
- ¼ cup tamari soy
- 1 tablespoon rice wine vinegar
- 3 tablespoons cornstarch dissolved in 1/4 cup water
- ¼ teaspoon Oriental sesame oil

Direction

- Coarsely chop the garlic, scallions and cilantro in a food processor. Scrape into a 14-by-11-by-2-inch ceramic dish. Stir in peanut oil. Cook, uncovered, at 100 percent for three minutes.
- Add the peppers. Cover tightly with microwave plastic wrap. Cook at 100 percent for five minutes.
- Uncover carefully and add the tomatoes. Re-cover tightly and cook at 100 percent for eight minutes.
- Uncover. Stir in the tamari soy, rice-wine vinegar and cornstarch mixture. Cook, uncovered, at 100 percent for four minutes. Stir in the sesame oil. Serve hot or cold.

Nutrition Information

- 76: calories;
- 3 grams: protein;
- 0 grams: saturated fat;
- 1 gram: polyunsaturated fat;
- 11 grams: carbohydrates;
- 5 grams: sugars;
- 9 milligrams: sodium;

51. Chinese Style Fish Fillets

Serving: 4 servings | Prep: | Cook: | Ready in: 20mins

Ingredients

- 1 pound Napa cabbage or bok choy, shredded (about 8 cups)
- ¼ cup peeled and slivered fresh ginger
- 1 pound skinned striped bass fillet, 1/2-inch thick
- ¼ cup water
- 1 teaspoon cornstarch
- 4 scallions, trimmed, white and green parts thinly sliced
- 2 tablespoons tamari soy sauce
- 4 teaspoons mirin (sweetened rice wine)
- 4 teaspoons rice wine vinegar
- 4 cloves garlic, smashed, peeled and minced
- 1 tablespoon peeled and grated ginger
- 2 teaspoons dark sesame oil
- 1 teaspoon chili oil

Direction

- In a bowl, toss the cabbage and slivered ginger together until ginger is evenly distributed. Arrange in the center of a rectangular dish 11by 7 by 2 inches. Score smooth side of fish fillet with slashes 1/8-inch deep and about 1 inch apart. Place fish, scored side up, over cabbage and ginger.
- Stir the water and cornstarch together until smooth. Stir in remaining ingredients and pour over fish.
- Cover tightly with microwave plastic wrap. Cook at 100 percent power in a high-power oven for 9 minutes. Prick plastic to release steam.
- Remove from oven and uncover.

Nutrition Information

- 189: calories;
- 24 grams: protein;
- 677 milligrams: sodium;
- 6 grams: fat;
- 1 gram: saturated fat;
- 0 grams: trans fat;
- 2 grams: sugars;
- 8 grams: carbohydrates;

52. Choco Hoto Pots

Serving: 4 servings | Prep: | Cook: | Ready in: 30mins

Ingredients

- Butter for ramekins
- ¾ cup semisweet chocolate chips
- 1 stick (4 ounces) unsalted butter
- 2 large eggs
- ¾ cup superfine sugar
- 3 tablespoons Italian 00 flour (see note) or all-purpose flour
- ½ cup white chocolate chips

Direction

- Place baking sheet in 400-degree oven. Butter four 2/3-cup ramekins and set aside.
- Using a microwave oven or double boiler, melt together the semisweet chocolate and the butter. Set aside to cool.
- In a separate bowl, combine eggs, sugar and flour. Add cooled chocolate mixture, and mix until blended. Fold in white chips.
- Divide mixture evenly among ramekins and place on baking sheet. Bake until tops are shiny and cracked and chocolate beneath is hot and gooey, about 20 minutes. Place each ramekin on a small plate with a teaspoon and serve, reminding children that ramekins and chocolate are hot.

Nutrition Information

- 684: calories;
- 44 grams: fat;
- 1 gram: trans fat;
- 74 grams: carbohydrates;
- 66 grams: sugars;
- 62 milligrams: sodium;
- 26 grams: saturated fat;
- 12 grams: monounsaturated fat;
- 2 grams: dietary fiber;
- 7 grams: protein;

53. Chocolate Cheesecake With Graham Cracker Crunch

Serving: 12 servings | Prep: | Cook: | Ready in: 2hours

Ingredients

- 2 cups/170 grams graham cracker crumbs
- ½ cup/100 grams light brown sugar
- 4 tablespoons/50 grams (1/2 stick) unsalted butter, melted
- 1 cup/250 milliliters sour cream
- 8 ounces/250 grams best-quality semisweet chocolate, preferably Callebaut, broken into pieces
- 1 ½ pounds/700 grams cream cheese
- 1 cup/200 grams granulated sugar
- 3 eggs
- To finish:
- 3 or 4 graham crackers
- 2 tablespoons/25 grams unsalted butter
- Chocolate ganache (optional; see recipe)

Direction

- Heat oven to 250 degrees. Line a 9- or 10-inch springform pan with parchment paper.
- In a bowl, combine graham cracker crumbs, brown sugar and melted butter, and use fingers to mix well. Press firmly into prepared pan, evenly covering the bottom and about 1/2 inch up the sides. Refrigerate until ready to bake.
- In a microwave or the top of a double boiler, heat sour cream and chocolate together just until chocolate is melted. Mix until smooth.
- In a mixer fitted with the paddle attachment, beat cream cheese and granulated sugar together until smooth and fluffy, at least 2 minutes. Mix in eggs one at a time. At low speed, gradually pour in chocolate mixture and mix until smooth.
- Pour filling over the crust in the pan and bake about 1 1/2 hours, until top is set and dry but still jiggles in the center when you shake the pan.
- Set aside to cool and refrigerate until ready to serve, up to 2 days.
- For garnish, place graham crackers in a thick sealable plastic bag and crush, using your hands or a pot, into irregular crumbs. In a small skillet, melt butter until it foams. Add crumbs and cook, stirring, until lightly toasted and fragrant.
- When ready to serve, gently remove sides of springform pan. Serve chilled cheesecake in slices, sprinkled with crumbs and drizzled with chocolate ganache (if using).

Nutrition Information

- 570: calories;
- 39 grams: fat;
- 21 grams: saturated fat;
- 4 grams: polyunsaturated fat;
- 52 grams: carbohydrates;
- 2 grams: dietary fiber;
- 7 grams: protein;
- 359 milligrams: sodium;
- 0 grams: trans fat;
- 11 grams: monounsaturated fat;
- 40 grams: sugars;

54. Chocolate Mug Cake

Serving: 1 serving | Prep: | Cook: | Ready in: 5mins

Ingredients

- 1 tablespoon unsalted butter
- 1 egg
- A few drops vanilla extract
- 3 to 4 tablespoons granulated sugar, to taste
- 3 tablespoons unsweetened cocoa powder
- A pinch of kosher salt
- 1 teaspoon mini chocolate chips (optional)
- Confectioners' sugar or vanilla ice cream (optional)

Direction

- Microwave the butter in a microwave-safe mug in 10-second increments until melted, 20 to 30 seconds. Crack the egg into a small bowl; add the vanilla and whisk to combine using a small whisk or fork. Pour the egg mixture into the mug over the butter and whisk to combine.
- Add the sugar, cocoa powder and salt and whisk until mostly smooth (a few lumps are O.K.). Scrape down the sides the best you can with a spoon or a small silicone spatula. Sprinkle with mini chocolate chips, if desired.
- Cook in the microwave on high for 1 to 1 1/2 minutes, or until a toothpick inserted in the center comes out mostly clean. Sift a little confectioners' sugar on top or serve with a scoop of vanilla ice cream, if desired. Dig in with a spoon.

Nutrition Information

- 371: calories;
- 9 grams: protein;
- 1 gram: polyunsaturated fat;
- 6 grams: dietary fiber;
- 5 grams: monounsaturated fat;
- 54 grams: carbohydrates;
- 44 grams: sugars;
- 184 milligrams: sodium;
- 18 grams: fat;
- 10 grams: saturated fat;
- 0 grams: trans fat;

55. Chocolate Orange Pudding

Serving: 8 servings | Prep: | Cook: | Ready in: 30mins

Ingredients

- Nonstick vegetable spray
- ½ cup slivered almonds
- Zest of 1/2 medium orange
- ½ cup light brown sugar
- ½ pound semisweet chocolate
- ½ teaspoon baking soda
- ¼ pound unsalted butter
- 3 large eggs
- ⅓ cup heavy cream
- 1 teaspoon Triple Sec

Direction

- Coat a 1 1/2-quart souffle dish with nonstick vegetable spray and reserve.
- Place almonds in the work bowl of a food processor, and process until finely chopped. Add orange zest and sugar, and finely chop again. Add chocolate, baking soda and butter, and process until smooth.
- Add eggs, cream and Triple Sec, and process until combined. Pour into prepared dish, and cover tightly with microwave plastic wrap. Cook at 100 percent power for 6 minutes. Prick plastic to release steam.
- Remove from oven, and uncover. Allow to stand; covered with a heavy plate, for 10 minutes.
- Unmold pudding onto serving plate, and serve warm.

Nutrition Information

- 378: calories;
- 3 grams: dietary fiber;
- 5 grams: protein;
- 15 grams: saturated fat;
- 30 grams: carbohydrates;
- 0 grams: trans fat;
- 10 grams: monounsaturated fat;
- 2 grams: polyunsaturated fat;
- 26 grams: sugars;
- 116 milligrams: sodium;
- 29 grams: fat;

56. Chocolate Sauce

Serving: About 1 cup | Prep: | Cook: | Ready in: 5mins

Ingredients

- 6 ounces bittersweet-chocolate pieces
- ½ cup heavy cream
- 1 tablespoon Grand Marnier

Direction

- Place chocolate and cream in a small microwave-safe bowl or pitcher. Cover with plastic wrap and microwave on high for 1 minute. Stir, return to the microwave and continue to cook in 10-second intervals until the chocolate is melted. Stir in the liqueur and serve, warm or at room temperature.

Nutrition Information

- 627: calories;
- 5 grams: protein;
- 32 milligrams: sodium;
- 48 grams: sugars;
- 29 grams: saturated fat;
- 15 grams: monounsaturated fat;
- 2 grams: polyunsaturated fat;
- 56 grams: carbohydrates;

57. Ciarla's Fish Soup

Serving: Four main portions or six first-course portions | Prep: | Cook: | Ready in: 1hours28mins

Ingredients

- ¼ pound slab bacon, cut into 1/4- by 1/4- by 1/2-inch pieces
- 1 tablespoon olive oil
- 1 tablespoon medium-hot paprika
- 1 cup chopped onion (about 1/2 large onion)
- 3 cloves garlic, smashed and peeled
- ½ cup dry white wine
- 2 cups fish broth (see Micro-Tips)
- 3 strips dry lasagna noodles, about 2 ounces, broken across into 1-inch pieces
- 8 littleneck clams (about 1 pound), scrubbed
- ½ cup tomato puree
- 4 mussels, scrubbed and debearded
- 1 cup canned pink beans, drained and rinsed
- ½ pound squid, cleaned, bodies sliced into rings, tentacles quartered, OR 1/2 pound bay scallops
- Pinch dried sage
- Pinch dried thyme
- Pinch freshly ground black pepper

Direction

- Place bacon in a 5-quart casserole. Cover loosely with paper toweling. Cook at 100 percent power for 7 minutes. Remove from oven and uncover.
- Remove bacon with a slotted spoon to paper toweling to drain; set aside. Pour off most of the fat from casserole, leaving about 1 tablespoon behind. Add oil and paprika and stir to make a paste. Mound in the center of casserole. Cook, uncovered, for 2 minutes.
- Remove from oven. Add onion and garlic and toss to coat. Cook, uncovered, for 2 minutes 30 seconds. Stir in wine, 1 1/2 cups of the fish broth and lasagna pieces. Cover securely with microwave plastic wrap or with a tightly fitting lid and cook for 5 minutes.
- If using plastic, prick plastic to release steam. Remove from oven and uncover. Arrange clams, hinge-end down around the inside edge of the dish. Re-cover and cook for 5 minutes or until clams open. Prick plastic to release steam.
- Remove from oven and uncover. Stir in tomato puree and arrange mussels, hinge-end down, in the center of the dish. Cover and cook for 5 minutes, or until mussels open.
- If using plastic, prick to release steam. Remove from oven and uncover. Add remaining ingredients and stir to combine. Cover and cook for 4 minutes or until squid is opaque. Remove from oven and uncover. Stir in bacon pieces and serve.

Nutrition Information

- 444: calories;

- 18 grams: fat;
- 5 grams: saturated fat;
- 0 grams: trans fat;
- 8 grams: monounsaturated fat;
- 3 grams: dietary fiber;
- 29 grams: carbohydrates;
- 4 grams: sugars;
- 35 grams: protein;
- 1585 milligrams: sodium;

58. Cold Borscht

Serving: Six servings | Prep: | Cook: |Ready in: 30mins

Ingredients

- 1 ½ pounds beets, washed and stems trimmed to about 1 inch
- 3 ½ cups vegetable broth (see recipe)
- ½ cup granulated sugar
- 3 tablespoons white vinegar
- ½ cup heavy cream
- ½ cup sour cream
- ½ cup buttermilk
- ¼ cup freshly squeezed lemon juice
- Kosher salt and freshly ground pepper to taste

Direction

- Place the beets in an 8-inch-by-8-inch-by-2-inch dish, with the smaller ones toward the center. Cover the dish tightly with microwave-safe plastic wrap. Cook the beets at 100 percent power in a 650- to 700-watt oven for 16 minutes. Prick the plastic to release the steam.
- Remove from the oven and uncover. Allow the beets to stand until cool.
- Wearing rubber gloves to prevent staining your hands, peel and grate the beets. Reserve.
- Combine the vegetable broth, sugar and vinegar in a two-and-one-half-quart souffle dish or casserole with a tightly fitting lid. Cover and cook at 100 percent power for three minutes.

- Remove from the oven and uncover. Stir to dissolve any remaining sugar. Stir in the reserved beets. Refrigerate until cool.
- Stir in the remaining ingredients and season. Refrigerate until ready to serve.

Nutrition Information

- 234: calories;
- 12 grams: fat;
- 3 grams: protein;
- 1 gram: polyunsaturated fat;
- 7 grams: saturated fat;
- 31 grams: carbohydrates;
- 4 grams: dietary fiber;
- 27 grams: sugars;
- 792 milligrams: sodium;

59. Cold Salmon With Gribiche

Serving: 8 servings | Prep: | Cook: |Ready in: 30mins

Ingredients

- 2 center-cut salmon fillets (each 1 3/4 pounds)
- 5 large eggs, hard boiled and peeled
- ¼ pound shallots, peeled and minced
- 1 ½ cups loosely packed parsley leaves, minced
- ⅔ cup loosely packed tarragon leaves, chopped fine
- ¼ cup capers, drained, rinsed and chopped coarse
- ½ cup olive oil
- ¼ cup fruity red wine vinegar
- ¾ teaspoon dry mustard
- 1 ½ teaspoons kosher salt
- ¼ teaspoon freshly ground pepper

Direction

- Place one piece of salmon, skin side down, in a 14-by-9-by-2-inch oval dish. Place second piece on top of first piece, skin side up, with the thicker side over the thinner side of the bottom fillet, so that the assembled fillets will be of even thickness.

- Cover with microwavable plastic wrap. Cook at 100 percent power in a high-power oven for 10 minutes. Prick plastic to release steam.
- Remove from oven and uncover. Let stand until cool enough to handle. Gently remove skin from top piece of salmon. Transfer salmon to a platter and refrigerate covered with a damp cloth until well chilled.
- To make the sauce, separate egg yolks from whites. Pass the yolks through a ricer and reserve. Finely chop the whites and place in a medium bowl.
- Add shallots, parsley, tarragon and capers to the bowl and stir to combine. Add remaining ingredients and stir well. Refrigerate.
- To serve, slice salmon across into 8 equal slices and spoon some of the sauce over each serving. Garnish with reserved yolk from sauce.

Nutrition Information

- 397: calories;
- 15 grams: monounsaturated fat;
- 1 gram: sugars;
- 26 grams: protein;
- 427 milligrams: sodium;
- 5 grams: carbohydrates;
- 30 grams: fat;
- 6 grams: polyunsaturated fat;
- 0 grams: trans fat;

60. Cooked Artichokes

Serving: | Prep: | Cook: | Ready in: 11mins

Ingredients

- 1 to 4 artichokes, 6 to 8 ounces each
- Lemon half

Direction

- Trim the artichoke with a serrated knife: cut the stem flush with the bottom of the artichoke; cut 1 inch off the top of the artichoke, and trim off the prickly leaf tips. As you work rub cut surfaces with the lemon half to keep them from discoloring.
- Place each artichoke in a microwave cooking bag, closing the bag tightly, or on a six-inch sheet of PV plastic wrap, folding the plastic to enclose the artichoke and sealing it tightly. Arrange the artichokes in a ring on the microwave carousel or on a large plate. Cook at 100 percent power (high setting). In a full-size oven (600 watts or more), one artichoke will take 9 minutes, two 11 minutes, and four 15 minutes. In a small oven (under 500 watts), one artichoke will take 12 minutes and two 20 minutes. Four won't fit in a small oven.
- To check for doneness, press the bottom of an artichoke with a fingernail; it should give. Remove from the oven. Let stand 5 minutes. Prick the plastic with a knife to release the steam. Unwrap carefully.

Nutrition Information

- 51: calories;
- 6 grams: dietary fiber;
- 1 gram: sugars;
- 3 grams: protein;
- 94 milligrams: sodium;
- 0 grams: polyunsaturated fat;
- 12 grams: carbohydrates;

61. Corn Chowder

Serving: 6 servings (7 cups) | Prep: | Cook: | Ready in: 32mins

Ingredients

- 1 pound baking potatoes, peeled and cut in 1/3-inch dice
- 1 medium red bell pepper, cored, de-ribbed and cut in 1/4-inch dice
- 1 medium green bell pepper, cored, de-ribbed and cut in 1/4-inch dice
- 1 small onion, chopped
- 1 cup water
- 4 ears corn, kernels removed from cob (2 cups), cooked
- 4 scallions, white and green parts, trimmed and thinly sliced
- 2 stalks celery, peeled and thinly sliced
- 1 ½ cups milk
- ½ cup heavy cream
- 1 tablespoon kosher salt
- 3 drops hot red pepper sauce
- Freshly ground pepper to taste
- 2 tablespoons unsalted butter, optional

Direction

- Place potatoes, peppers, onion and water in a 5-quart casserole dish with a tightly fitting lid. Cook, covered, at 100 percent power in a high-power oven for 12 minutes.
- Stir in corn, scallions, celery, milk and cream. Cook, covered, for 9 minutes.
- Remove from oven. Stir in salt, pepper sauce and black pepper. Cool slightly before serving. Stir in butter if desired.

Nutrition Information

- 247: calories;
- 6 grams: saturated fat;
- 0 grams: trans fat;
- 3 grams: monounsaturated fat;
- 4 grams: dietary fiber;
- 7 grams: protein;
- 790 milligrams: sodium;
- 10 grams: fat;
- 1 gram: polyunsaturated fat;
- 35 grams: carbohydrates;
- 11 grams: sugars;

62. Corn Fritters

Serving: 25 to 30 fritters | Prep: | Cook: | Ready in: 31mins

Ingredients

- 4 ears fresh corn, shucked and silk removed
- 2 tablespoons granulated sugar
- 2 teaspoons kosher salt
- Pinch of paprika
- Freshly ground black pepper to taste
- 3 cups vegetable oil
- 3 eggs, separated
- ¼ cup sifted all-purpose flour
- ½ teaspoon baking powder
- Nectarine sauce (see recipe), maple syrup or creme fraiche and caviar

Direction

- Score corn through middle of each kernel with a sharp knife. Grate corn from cob or cut kernels from cob with a very sharp knife (do not cut so deeply as to include part of cob). Put kernels in a 4-cup glass or ceramic bowl. Mash slightly with a potato masher until a milky liquid is exuded. Add sugar, salt, paprika and pepper and stir. Cover tightly with polyvinyl microwave plastic wrap. Cook at 100 percent 1 minute. Uncover and stir. Reserve.
- In an 8-cup measure, heat oil at 100 percent 15 minutes, until a microwave thermometer registers 375 degrees Fahrenheit. To the corn, add egg yolks, flour and baking powder and stir. Beat egg whites until stiff. Fold into corn mixture.
- Drop corn mixture by the tablespoon into hot oil. Depending upon shape of measuring cup, you will be able to cook 6 to 10 fritters at a time. Cook, uncovered, 45 seconds at 100 percent. Turn fritters over with a slotted spoon. Cook 45 seconds longer, until fritters are golden brown. Remove and drain on paper towel.

- Heat oil at 100 percent 5 minutes between batches. Continue making fritters with remaining batter. Do not remove container of oil from microwave oven until it cools. Serve fritters immediately with nectarine sauce, maple syrup or creme fraiche and caviar.

Nutrition Information

- 239: calories;
- 2 grams: sugars;
- 1 gram: protein;
- 106 milligrams: sodium;
- 25 grams: fat;
- 0 grams: dietary fiber;
- 18 grams: monounsaturated fat;
- 4 grams: polyunsaturated fat;
- 5 grams: carbohydrates;

63. Corn And Black Bean Salad

Serving: 3 cups | Prep: | Cook: | Ready in: 15mins

Ingredients

- 1 cup cooked corn kernels (see Micro-Tips)
- 1 cup canned black beans, thoroughly rinsed and drained, or 1 cup dried beans cooked
- 8 to 9 ounces ripe tomato, cored and cut 1/4-inch dice (1 cup)
- 1 ½ ounces peeled onion, finely diced
- 1 cup lightly packed cilantro leaves, coarsely chopped
- 1 to 2 jalapeno peppers, fresh or canned, seeded and very finely chopped
- 2 tablespoons lime juice
- 2 tablespoons olive oil
- 1 teaspoon kosher salt, or more if using home-cooked beans
- Freshly ground pepper to taste

Direction

- Combine all ingredients. Allow to stand for 1/2 hour. Taste for salt and pepper.

Nutrition Information

- 185: calories;
- 4 grams: sugars;
- 6 grams: protein;
- 90 milligrams: sodium;
- 8 grams: fat;
- 1 gram: polyunsaturated fat;
- 25 grams: carbohydrates;
- 5 grams: monounsaturated fat;
- 7 grams: dietary fiber;

64. Couscous Risotto

Serving: 8 cups | Prep: | Cook: | Ready in: 25mins

Ingredients

- ½ cup olive oil
- 1 medium-size onion, minced
- 10 medium-size garlic cloves, smashed, peeled and minced
- 3 tablespoons ground cumin, preferably freshly ground
- 1 tablespoon curry powder
- 2 cups couscous
- 4 cups chicken broth or vegetarian broth (see Micro-Tip)
- 1 ½ teaspoons kosher salt
- Freshly ground black pepper

Direction

- Place oil in a 14- by 9- by 2-inch oval dish. Cook, uncovered, at 100 percent in a high-power oven for 2 minutes. Stir in onion and garlic. Cook for 2 minutes. Stir in spices and cook for 3 minutes.
- Stir in couscous and pour broth over mixture. Cook for 10 minutes.
- Remove from oven. Stir in salt and pepper.

Nutrition Information

- 245: calories;
- 2 grams: saturated fat;
- 8 grams: monounsaturated fat;
- 3 grams: dietary fiber;
- 305 milligrams: sodium;
- 12 grams: fat;
- 1 gram: sugars;
- 30 grams: carbohydrates;
- 5 grams: protein;

65. Crabmeat Tostadas

Serving: 6 main-dish servings or 10 appetizer servings. | Prep: | Cook: | Ready in: 10mins

Ingredients

- 1 pound cooked crabmeat, picked over for shells
- 1 to 2 jalapeño or serrano chilies, seeded if desired and minced
- 4 scallions, white and light green parts, sliced thin or minced
- ½ pound tomatoes, finely diced (optional; omit if good tomatoes are not available)
- ⅔ cup corn kernels (fresh or thawed frozen), steamed for 5 minutes
- ¼ cup chopped cilantro
- ¼ cup fresh lime juice (more to taste)
- 2 tablespoons extra virgin olive oil (optional)
- Salt to taste
- 9 corn tortillas, cut into quarters or halves and toasted in the microwave
- Sliced radishes (optional)

Direction

- Toss together all of the ingredients except the tortillas and radishes. If desired, warm through in a pan over medium heat, but don't cook the crab, or it will become too tough.

- Spoon the crab mixture onto the toasted tortilla halves or triangles. Garnish with radish slices if desired and serve.

Nutrition Information

- 175: calories;
- 17 grams: protein;
- 447 milligrams: sodium;
- 2 grams: sugars;
- 0 grams: monounsaturated fat;
- 1 gram: polyunsaturated fat;
- 23 grams: carbohydrates;
- 4 grams: dietary fiber;

66. Cranberry Beans With Tomatoes And Herbs

Serving: 10 to 12 servings | Prep: | Cook: | Ready in: 1hours15mins

Ingredients

- ¼ cup olive oil
- 1 large onion, halved lengthwise and cut across in thin slices
- 3 ½ pounds cranberry beans, shelled and soaked in water at least 1 hour, or 3 19-ounce cans cannellini beans, drained and rinsed (see note)
- 2 ¼ pounds tomatoes, cored and cut in 1 1/4-inch chunks
- 6 to 8 fresh sage leaves, chopped fine
- 1 large sprig summer savory or 1 teaspoon dried
- Kosher salt and freshly ground black pepper to taste

Direction

- Place olive oil in a 5-quart casserole with a tight-fitting lid. Cook, uncovered, at 100 percent power in a high-power oven for 2 minutes. Add onions and stir to coat with oil. Cook, uncovered, for 4 minutes.

- Drain beans and stir them in. Cook, uncovered, for 3 minutes. Stir in tomatoes, sage and savory. Cook, covered, for 45 minutes, stirring twice.
- Remove from oven and uncover. Season with salt and pepper. Cook, covered, for 7 minutes to reheat.

Nutrition Information

- 174: calories;
- 8 grams: protein;
- 548 milligrams: sodium;
- 5 grams: fat;
- 1 gram: polyunsaturated fat;
- 3 grams: sugars;
- 25 grams: carbohydrates;
- 10 grams: dietary fiber;

67. Cranberry Cassis Mold

Serving: One 4 3/4-cup mold | Prep: | Cook: | Ready in: 25mins

Ingredients

- 1 ½ cups cassis syrup (not liquor or juice)
- ½ cup water
- ¾ cup granulated sugar
- 1 ½ pounds fresh cranberries (6 cups)

Direction

- Combine all ingredients in a 2 1/2-quart souffle dish with a tight-fitting lid. Cook, covered, at 100 percent power in a high-power oven for 10 minutes.
- Uncover and stir well. Cook, uncovered, for 10 minutes.
- Remove from oven. Rinse a metal bowl or mold with ice water. Pour in cranberry mixture. Allow to cool. Cover with plastic wrap and refrigerate overnight.

- Just before serving, dip mold into a bowl of hot water for a few seconds and jiggle slightly to loosen. Invert onto a serving platter or into the well of a dinner plate.

68. Cranberry Pistachio Chutney With Figs

Serving: 3 cups | Prep: | Cook: | Ready in: 15mins

Ingredients

- 1 12-ounce package fresh cranberries, picked clean
- 1 orange, skin intact and seeds discarded, chopped into 1/4-inch cubes
- 2 tablespoons lemon juice
- 2 tablespoons finely chopped shallots
- 1 teaspoon dry ginger powder
- 1 cup sugar
- ¾ teaspoon coarse salt
- ½ teaspoon ground cinnamon
- 1 teaspoon ground cumin
- ⅓ teaspoon cayenne
- 1 teaspoon mustard seeds, lightly crushed
- ⅓ cup shelled unsalted pistachio nuts (preferably raw)
- ⅔ cup California black figs, stemmed and chopped into 1/2-inch pieces, or 2/3 cup dark raisins

Direction

- Combine all the ingredients except the pistachios and figs in a 2 1/2-quart microwave-proof casserole dish and cover. Cook at 100 percent power in a 650- to 700-watt microwave carousel oven for 4 minutes. Uncover and continue cooking for an additional 5 minutes, or until the chutney is boiling and the cranberries begin to burst open. Stir once during the cooking time.
- Remove from the oven. Stir in the pistachios and figs or raisins. Replace the cover and set aside to cool completely. Spoon the chutney

into sterilized jars, cover and refrigerate. (For best results, let the chutney ripen for at least a day. If refrigerated and tightly covered, it will keep for several months.) Serve with grilled chicken, roast pork or turkey or on toast for breakfast.

Nutrition Information

- 260: calories;
- 4 grams: fat;
- 1 gram: polyunsaturated fat;
- 59 grams: carbohydrates;
- 5 grams: dietary fiber;
- 48 grams: sugars;
- 3 grams: protein;
- 240 milligrams: sodium;
- 2 grams: monounsaturated fat;
- 0 grams: saturated fat;

69. Creamy Carrot Soup

Serving: 4 cups | Prep: | Cook: | Ready in: 20mins

Ingredients

- ¾ pound carrots, peeled, trimmed and cut into 1-inch lengths
- 2 ¾ cups chicken broth, homemade or canned
- 1 ½ teaspoons ground cumin
- 1 cup part skim-milk ricotta cheese
- 1 teaspoon kosher salt, or less if using canned broth
- 1 tablespoon fresh lemon juice

Direction

- Place the carrots, 3/4 cup broth and the cumin in a 9-inch pie plate. Cover tightly with microwave plastic wrap. Cook at 100 percent power in a 650-watt to 700-watt oven for 15 minutes, until the carrots are easily pierced with the tip of a knife.

- Place the ricotta in a blender with 1/4 cup of the broth. Blend until smooth.
- Remove the carrots from the oven. Prick the plastic to release steam and uncover. Add to the blender and blend until smooth.
- Scrape the carrot mixture into a serving bowl. Whisk in the remaining broth and salt. If serving hot, cover and reheat at 100 percent power for 4 minutes and then add lemon juice. If serving chilled, stir in lemon juice and chill in the refrigerator for 3 hours or overnight.

Nutrition Information

- 206: calories;
- 348 milligrams: sodium;
- 6 grams: saturated fat;
- 1 gram: polyunsaturated fat;
- 2 grams: dietary fiber;
- 7 grams: sugars;
- 12 grams: protein;
- 10 grams: fat;
- 3 grams: monounsaturated fat;
- 16 grams: carbohydrates;

70. Creamy Lobster Sauce

Serving: None | Prep: | Cook: | Ready in:

Ingredients

- 2 1 1/4-pound live lobsters, rinsed in cold water
- 3 tablespoons unsalted butter
- ¼ pound onion, peeled and minced
- 1 tablespoon Worcestershire sauce
- 1 teaspoon Dijon-style mustard
- ½ teaspoon hot red pepper sauce, like Tabasco
- 1 cup heavy cream
- ½ cup chicken broth
- 2 tablespoons chopped fresh tarragon leaves
- 2 tablespoons freshly squeezed lemon juice, or to taste
- Coarse kosher salt to taste

- Freshly ground black pepper to taste

Direction

- In a large, microwave-safe plastic bag, arrange lobsters head to tail. Twist the top of the bag shut. Cook in a 650- to 700-watt oven at 100 percent power for 8 minutes. Carefully remove from oven. Drain any liquid that has collected in the bag into a bowl. Remove lobsters from bag and allow to cool while proceeding with the recipe.
- In a 2-quart souffle dish, melt butter, uncovered, at 100 percent power for 2 minutes. Stir in onion and cook, uncovered, at 100 percent power for 3 minutes. Remove from oven. Whisk in Worcestershire, mustard and Tabasco. Set aside.
- Holding the lobster over the bowl, separate the head from the body. Using a spoon, scrape out tomalley and roe into the bowl, being careful to avoid the brain sac. Holding the feelers, squeeze the head to extract juices. Remove meat from tail and claws. Dice the tails. Reserve claws whole for garnishing.
- Add cream and chicken broth to onion/butter mixture. Heat, uncovered, at 100 percent power for 4 minutes. Whisk tomalley, roe and reserved juices into cream mixture. Cook, uncovered, at 100 percent power for 4 minutes. Add tarragon and reserved lobster tail meat and cook 2 minutes longer. Remove from oven. Season to taste with lemon juice, salt and pepper. Toss with hot fettucine. Garnish with reserved claws. Serve immediately.

Nutrition Information

- 356: calories;
- 6 grams: monounsaturated fat;
- 1 gram: dietary fiber;
- 5 grams: carbohydrates;
- 3 grams: sugars;
- 22 grams: fat;
- 13 grams: saturated fat;
- 0 grams: trans fat;

- 33 grams: protein;
- 885 milligrams: sodium;

71. Creamy Oyster Soup

Serving: Eight first-course portions | Prep: | Cook: | Ready in: 33mins

Ingredients

- 3 dozen oysters, shucked in their liquid
- 4 cups fish broth (see Micro-Tips)
- 1 pound potatoes (2 large potatoes), peeled and cut into 1/4-inch cubes
- 1 cup heavy cream
- ¾ vial thread saffron, about 1#3 gram
- 1 bunch scallions, thinly sliced across (about 1 cup)
- 1 teaspoon kosher salt

Direction

- Place oysters in a strainer set over a large bowl to catch liquid.
- Combine potatoes and broth in a 5-quart casserole. Cover tightly with microwave plastic wrap. Cook at 100 percent power in a 650- to 700-watt oven for 15 minutes or until potatoes are tender.
- Prick plastic to release steam. Remove from oven and uncover. Add oyster liquid, cream and saffron. Cover tightly with microwave plastic wrap and cook for 7 minutes.
- Pick plastic to release steam. Remove from oven and uncover. Cut each oyster in half with a kitchen scissors. Add to soup with scallions and salt. Cook, uncovered, for 1 minute.
- Remove from oven and let stand for several minutes. Serve hot

Nutrition Information

- 379: calories;
- 4 grams: monounsaturated fat;
- 2 grams: sugars;

- 26 grams: protein;
- 880 milligrams: sodium;
- 30 grams: carbohydrates;
- 17 grams: fat;
- 8 grams: saturated fat;
- 3 grams: polyunsaturated fat;

---

72. Curried Onion Soup

Serving: 6 servings (7 cups) | Prep: | Cook: | Ready in: 45mins

Ingredients

- 2 ¼ pounds onions, peeled and cut in chunks
- ½ pound unsalted butter, cut in 1/2-inch pieces
- ¼ cup curry powder
- 4 cups chicken broth
- 3 tablespoons fresh lime juice
- 1 ½ teaspoons kosher salt

Direction

- Working in two batches, put onions in a food processor. Pulse until chopped medium fine. Set aside.
- Put butter in a 5-quart casserole with a tight-fitting lid. Cook, uncovered, at 100 percent power in a high-power microwave oven for 2 minutes.
- Stir in onions and curry powder until well coated with butter. Cover and cook for 30 minutes, stirring once.
- Remove from oven and uncover. Working in two batches, scrape mixture into a blender. Process until very smooth, stopping from time to time to scrape down sides of container.
- Scrape mixture back into casserole. Stir in broth. Cover and cook for 6 minutes, to heat through. Remove from oven and whisk in lime juice and salt.

Nutrition Information

- 412: calories;
- 10 grams: sugars;
- 20 grams: saturated fat;
- 1 gram: trans fat;
- 9 grams: monounsaturated fat;
- 2 grams: polyunsaturated fat;
- 25 grams: carbohydrates;
- 5 grams: dietary fiber;
- 712 milligrams: sodium;
- 33 grams: fat;
- 7 grams: protein;

---

73. Curried Tomato Soup

Serving: 4 servings | Prep: | Cook: | Ready in: 16mins

Ingredients

- 2 tablespoons unsalted butter
- 1 small onion, peeled and finely chopped
- 3 tablespoons curry powder
- 1 tablespoon sweet paprika
- 1 ¾ cups plum tomato sauce (see Micro-Tip)
- 2 cups chicken broth
- 2 tablespoons fresh lemon juice
- 2 teaspoons kosher salt
- Freshly ground black pepper to taste
- ¼ cup lowfat yogurt, optional

Direction

- Place butter in a 2 1/2-quart souffle dish with a tightly fitting lid. Cook, uncovered, at 100 percent power in a high-power oven for 2 minutes. Stir in onion. Cook, uncovered, for 2 minutes.
- Stir in curry powder and paprika. Cook, uncovered, for 2 minutes.
- Remove from oven. Stir in tomato sauce. Whisk in chicken broth. Cook, covered, for 5 minutes.
- Remove from oven and uncover. Stir in lemon juice, salt and pepper. Ladle into bowls. Top each serving with 1 tablespoon yogurt, if desired.

Nutrition Information

- 151: calories;
- 3 grams: monounsaturated fat;
- 1 gram: polyunsaturated fat;
- 16 grams: carbohydrates;
- 5 grams: dietary fiber;
- 7 grams: sugars;
- 685 milligrams: sodium;
- 8 grams: fat;
- 4 grams: saturated fat;
- 0 grams: trans fat;
- 6 grams: protein;

74. Demitasse Carrot Custards

Serving: Eight custards | Prep: | Cook: |Ready in: 15mins

Ingredients

- ½ pound carrots, trimmed, peeled and cut into 1/4-inch round slices
- 4 large eggs
- ¾ cup heavy cream
- 1 teaspoon kosher salt
- ¾ teaspoon ground cumin

Direction

- Place the carrots in a one-and-a-half-quart souffle dish. Cover dish tightly with microwave plastic wrap. Cook at 100 percent for six minutes, 30 seconds.
- Uncover. Place the carrots in a blender. Add one egg and blend to a smooth puree. Add the remaining eggs one at a time, scraping down the sides of the blender after each addition. Pour into a clean bowl and stir in the cream, salt and cumin (you will have about two cups of custard).
- Divide the mixture evenly among eight demitasse cups. Cover each tightly with microwave plastic wrap. Arrange in a ring, not touching, on the microwave carousel or a 12-inch round platter. Cook at 100 percent for two minutes, 30 seconds, or until just set.
- Before removing the custards from the oven, pierce the plastic with the tip of a sharp knife so the plastic doesn't settle on the delicate custard surface.
- Remove from oven. Uncover (unmold if desired) and serve with a dollop of parsley sauce and a leaf of fresh parsley.

Nutrition Information

- 125: calories;
- 3 grams: monounsaturated fat;
- 1 gram: dietary fiber;
- 4 grams: protein;
- 2 grams: sugars;
- 176 milligrams: sodium;
- 11 grams: fat;
- 6 grams: saturated fat;
- 0 grams: trans fat;

75. Dhanshak (Parsi Cornish Hens Braised In Spiced Pumpkin Lentil Puree)

Serving: Six servings | Prep: | Cook: |Ready in: 40mins

Ingredients

- ¾ cup masar dal (red lentils), picked clean and rinsed
- 2 ½ cups water
- 1 teaspoon ground coriander
- 1 teaspoon ground cumin
- 1 teaspoon ground fennel
- 1 teaspoon cayenne, or more to taste
- 1 ½ teaspoons turmeric
- 2 teaspoons coarse salt
- ¼ cup fresh mint leaves, loosely packed

- ¼ cup fresh cilantro, loosely packed, or 2 tablespoons dried coriander leaves
- 1 1-inch cube fresh ginger, peeled and chopped coarse
- 4 large cloves garlic, peeled and chopped coarse
- 3 Cornish hens, skinned, trimmed of excess fat and halved, or 1 3 1/2-pound chicken, cut into 6 to 8 pieces
- 1 ½ cups chopped eggplant, skin on
- 1 ½ cups peeled, seeded pumpkin or butternut squash, cut into 1-inch pieces
- 1 cup chopped onion
- 3 tablespoons chopped fresh cilantro for garnish

Direction

- Layer all of the above ingredients, in the order listed, in a 5-quart microwave-proof casserole dish. Cover and cook at 100 percent power in a 650- to 700-watt microwave carousel oven for 35 minutes, or until the Cornish hens are tender and the lentils soft. Remove from the oven.
- Remove the hens and arrange them in a heated deep serving dish. Cover with aluminum foil to keep them warm.
- Meanwhile, transfer the vegetables and their liquid to a food processor and puree. You may have to work in batches. Do not overprocess: a little texture adds to the character of the sauce. Pour the sauce over the hens. Garnish with the fresh cilantro and serve.

Nutrition Information

- 470: calories;
- 7 grams: saturated fat;
- 0 grams: trans fat;
- 11 grams: monounsaturated fat;
- 5 grams: dietary fiber;
- 24 grams: fat;
- 26 grams: carbohydrates;
- 3 grams: sugars;
- 36 grams: protein;

- 744 milligrams: sodium;

76. Dividend Soup

Serving: 4 cups | Prep: | Cook: | Ready in: 30mins

Ingredients

- 1 ½ pounds celery root, trimmed, peeled and cut in1/2-inch cubes (3 cups)
- 1 tablespoon water
- 1 ¾ to 2 ¾ cups liquid reserved from puree for pumpkin-squash
- 1 cup chicken broth, or as much as is needed to bring liquid to 2 3/4 cups total
- ½ cup heavy cream
- 1 tablespoon kosher salt
- Freshly ground black pepper to taste
- Freshly grated nutmeg, optional

Direction

- Place celery root and water in a 4-cup measure. Cover tightly with microwavable plastic wrap. Cook in a 650- to 700-watt oven at 100 percent power for 14 minutes. Prick plastic to release steam.
- Remove from oven. Uncover. Puree the celery root in a food processor. Scrape into a medium saucepan.
- Whisk in pumpkin or squash liquid, and chicken broth if needed, cream, salt and pepper. Place over medium heat on stove and cook until heated through. Sprinkle nutmeg over each serving, if desired.

Nutrition Information

- 192: calories;
- 1 gram: polyunsaturated fat;
- 18 grams: carbohydrates;
- 5 grams: protein;
- 12 grams: fat;
- 7 grams: saturated fat;

- 3 grams: dietary fiber;
- 643 milligrams: sodium;
- 4 grams: monounsaturated fat;

77. Eggplant Dip

Serving: 1 1/2 cups, to serve six as an appetizer | Prep: | Cook: | Ready in: 18mins

Ingredients

- 1 pound eggplant, cooked as in Micro Tip
- ¼ cup tahini
- 3 tablespoons fresh lemon juice
- 1 teaspoon kosher salt
- 2 medium-size cloves garlic, smashed and peeled
- ½ jalapeno pepper, stemmed and seeded
- 1 tablespoon sesame seeds, optional

Direction

- Halve eggplant and scrape flesh from skin. Add flesh to remaining ingredients, except sesame seeds, in a food processor. Pulse until well combined. Stir in sesame seeds if desired.

Nutrition Information

- 163: calories;
- 2 grams: saturated fat;
- 15 grams: carbohydrates;
- 7 grams: dietary fiber;
- 6 grams: sugars;
- 441 milligrams: sodium;
- 11 grams: fat;
- 4 grams: monounsaturated fat;
- 5 grams: protein;

78. Eggplant And Tomato Casserole

Serving: 8 first-course servings | Prep: | Cook: | Ready in: 48mins

Ingredients

- 2 medium-size eggplants (about 14 ounces each), trimmed and cut crosswise into 1/4-inch slices
- 3 ½ teaspoons kosher salt
- 1 cup loosely packed basil leaves, cut crosswise into thin strips
- 4 medium-size tomatoes, cut crosswise in 1/4-inch slices
- 1 medium-size clove garlic, smashed, peeled and minced
- 3 teaspoons olive oil
- Freshly ground black pepper
- ¾ pound mozzarella, grated

Direction

- Place one-third of the eggplant slices in an even layer in a 14-by-9-by-2-inch oval dish. Sprinkle with 1 teaspoon of the salt. Cook, uncovered, at 100 percent power in a high-power oven for 10 minutes.
- Remove from oven. Rinse eggplant slices and pat dry.
- Repeat Steps 1 and 2 twice, with remaining eggplant slices.
- Rinse and dry dish. Arrange half the eggplant in a single layer in the bottom of the dish. Sprinkle with half the basil and half the garlic. Arrange half the tomato slices over the basil and garlic. Drizzle with half the olive oil. Sprinkle with 1/4 teaspoon salt and pepper. Cover with half the mozzarella. Repeat the layers.
- Cook, uncovered, at 100 percent power in a high-power oven for 8 minutes.
- Remove from oven. Spoon the accumulated juices over the top.

Nutrition Information

- 176: calories;
- 9 grams: carbohydrates;
- 11 grams: protein;
- 486 milligrams: sodium;
- 1 gram: polyunsaturated fat;
- 4 grams: monounsaturated fat;
- 3 grams: dietary fiber;
- 5 grams: sugars;
- 12 grams: fat;
- 6 grams: saturated fat;

79. Emily Nathan's Marrow Balls

Serving: About 20 marrow balls | Prep: | Cook: | Ready in: 30mins

Ingredients

- 4 tablespoons marrow (from about 1 1/2 pounds marrow bones)
- 3 large eggs, well beaten
- 1 teaspoon salt, or to taste
- Dash of grated nutmeg
- 1 tablespoon chopped parsley
- ½ cup matzoh meal

Direction

- To remove the marrow from the bones, place them on a paper towel or plate in a microwave for 40 seconds. Scrape the bone with a spoon or a table knife and reserve 4 tablespoons of the marrow.
- In a bowl, cream the marrow with a fork until perfectly smooth. Mix in the eggs, salt, nutmeg and chopped parsley. Mix in enough matzoh meal to make a soft dough. Cover the bowl with plastic wrap and set aside for several hours in the refrigerator.
- Using your hands, roll the dough into balls the size of a quarter. Meanwhile, bring the chicken soup to a simmer. Fill a separate saucepan with water and bring it to a boil. Drop in one

marrow ball; if it doesn't hold together, add more matzoh meal to the dough.
- Test again. When the test ball holds together, drop the remaining balls into the simmering soup and cook 10 to 15 minutes or until light and cooked through.

Nutrition Information

- 41: calories;
- 1 gram: protein;
- 28 milligrams: sodium;
- 3 grams: fat;
- 0 grams: sugars;

80. Festive Fish Fillets

Serving: 2 servings | Prep: | Cook: | Ready in: 18mins

Ingredients

- 2 6-ounce fish fillets, 1/2 inch thick (flounder, sole or similar fish)
- ½ teaspoon fresh lemon juice
- 1 cup diced red bell pepper (about 8 ounces)
- 2 tablespoons snipped chives
- Pinch hot red pepper flakes
- 1 tablespoon chopped fresh cilantro (optional)
- 4 ounces broccoli florets, cut into very small pieces, about 1 inch in diameter
- Kosher salt

Direction

- Put one fish fillet in the center of each dinner plate. Sprinkle fish with lemon juice.
- Stir together red bell pepper, chives, red pepper flakes and cilantro.
- Place half of the pepper mixture in a stripe down the center of each fillet. Arrange broccoli on either side of fillets. Cover tightly with microwave plastic wrap. Using a rack, cook for 3 minutes, switching plates from top to bottom after 1 minute 30 seconds.

- Pierce plastic wrap on each plate. Remove wrap. Wipe up liquid if desired. Serve immediately.

Nutrition Information

- 206: calories;
- 3 grams: fat;
- 1 gram: polyunsaturated fat;
- 10 grams: carbohydrates;
- 2 grams: dietary fiber;
- 5 grams: sugars;
- 35 grams: protein;
- 778 milligrams: sodium;

81. Fish Broth

Serving: 3 1/2 cups | Prep: | Cook: |Ready in: P2DT40mins

Ingredients

- 2 pounds fish heads and bones, cleaned of any blood and cut into 2- inch pieces

Direction

- Combine the fish and four cups of cold water in a five-quart casserole with a tightly fitting lid. Cook, covered, at 100 percent power in a 650- to 700-watt oven for 30 minutes.
- Remove from the oven and uncover. If just the broth is required, strain through a fine sieve and discard the heads and bones. Store, covered, in the refrigerator for up to two days, or freeze. If proceeding with the soup, pass the broth with all the solids through a food mill with a medium blade. Discard the pulp and reserve the broth for the soup.

Nutrition Information

- 17: calories;
- 0 grams: polyunsaturated fat;

- 4 grams: protein;
- 9 milligrams: sodium;

82. Fish And Vegetables

Serving: 4 servings | Prep: | Cook: |Ready in: 15mins

Ingredients

- 1 pound boneless swordfish or tuna steak, about 1/2-inch thick
- 2 teaspoons kosher salt
- 4 ounces mushrooms, wiped clean with a damp cloth and thinly sliced lengthwise (about 2 cups)
- 2 cups broccoli florets
- 4 ounces green beans, trimmed and quartered crosswise (about 1 1/3 cups)
- 4 ounces carrots, cut into 1-inch-thick matchsticks (about 1 1/3 cups)
- ¼ cup fresh lemon juice
- 2 tablespoons olive oil
- Freshly ground black pepper to taste
- 1 ½ tablespoons chopped fresh herbs, such as mint, dill or parsley

Direction

- Place fish in the center of an oval dish 14 by 9 by 2 inches. Sprinkle with salt. Top with the mushrooms and broccoli. Arrange green beans and carrots around the fish.
- Mix lemon juice, oil, pepper and herbs together in a small bowl. Pour over the fish and vegetables.
- Cover tightly with microwave plastic wrap. Cook at 100 percent power in a high-power oven for 8 minutes, or until carrots are cooked. Prick plastic to release steam.
- Remove from oven and uncover. Serve hot.

Nutrition Information

- 229: calories;

- 629 milligrams: sodium;
- 8 grams: fat;
- 1 gram: polyunsaturated fat;
- 0 grams: trans fat;
- 5 grams: monounsaturated fat;
- 2 grams: dietary fiber;
- 31 grams: protein;
- 10 grams: carbohydrates;
- 4 grams: sugars;

83. Fresh Herb Butter

Serving: Enough for 6 ears of corn | Prep: | Cook: | Ready in: 30mins

Ingredients

- 7 tablespoons unsalted butter, cut into tablespoon-size pieces
- 2 tablespoons fresh tarragon leaves, chopped
- 2 tablespoons chopped fresh chives
- 2 tablespoons fresh thyme leaves
- 2 tablespoons fresh lemon juice
- Freshly ground black pepper to taste

Direction

- Put 6 tablespoons butter into a 4-cup glass measuring cup. Cook, uncovered, at 100 percent 20 seconds to soften. 2.Remove from oven. Beat in remaining ingredients, including remaining butter.

Nutrition Information

- 125: calories;
- 14 grams: fat;
- 9 grams: saturated fat;
- 1 gram: carbohydrates;
- 3 grams: monounsaturated fat;
- 0 grams: protein;
- 3 milligrams: sodium;

84. Fresh Tuna In Tomato Rhubarb Sauce

Serving: 4 to 6 servings | Prep: | Cook: | Ready in: 22mins

Ingredients

- 2 pounds tuna, 2 inches thick, cut in 2-by-1 1/2-inch chunks
- 1 ¼ pounds rhubarb, trimmed and cut on the diagonal in 1/8-inch slices (3 cups)
- 1 cup Italian chopped tomatoes, or 1 cup peeled, seeded and chopped ripe tomatoes
- ½ cup red wine
- 2 tablespoons olive oil
- 2 tablespoons honey
- ½ teaspoon kosher salt
- Freshly ground black pepper to taste

Direction

- Place tuna in a single layer in a 5-quart casserole with a tight-fitting lid. Place rhubarb evenly over tuna. Cover with tomatoes, wine, olive oil and honey.
- Cook, covered, at 100 percent power in a high-power oven for 15 minutes.
- Remove from oven and uncover. Stir in salt and pepper.

Nutrition Information

- 260: calories;
- 5 grams: fat;
- 1 gram: polyunsaturated fat;
- 0 grams: trans fat;
- 7 grams: sugars;
- 38 grams: protein;
- 3 grams: monounsaturated fat;
- 10 grams: carbohydrates;
- 2 grams: dietary fiber;
- 230 milligrams: sodium;

85. From Beans To Apples Cranberry Beans With Tomatoes And Herbs

Serving: 10 - 12 servings | Prep: | Cook: |Ready in: 1hours15mins

Ingredients

- ¼ cup olive oil
- 1 large onion, halved lengthwise and cut across in thin slices
- 3 ½ pounds cranberry beans, shelled and soaked in water at least 1 hour, or 3 19-ounce cans cannellini beans, drained and rinsed (see note)
- 2 ¼ pounds tomatoes, cored and cut in 1 1/4-inch chunks
- 6 to 8 fresh sage leaves, chopped fine
- 1 large sprig summer savory or 1 teaspoon dried
- Kosher salt and freshly ground black pepper to taste

Direction

- Place olive oil in a 5-quart casserole with a tight-fitting lid. Cook, uncovered, at 100 percent power in a high-power oven for 2 minutes. Add onions and stir to coat with oil. Cook, uncovered, for 4 minutes.
- Drain beans and stir them in. Cook, uncovered, for 3 minutes. Stir in tomatoes, sage and savory. Cook, covered, for 45 minutes, stirring twice.
- Remove from oven and uncover. Season with salt and pepper. Cook, covered, for 7 minutes to reheat.

Nutrition Information

- 174: calories;
- 1 gram: polyunsaturated fat;
- 3 grams: sugars;
- 25 grams: carbohydrates;
- 10 grams: dietary fiber;
- 8 grams: protein;
- 548 milligrams: sodium;
- 5 grams: fat;

86. Frozen Apricot Mousse

Serving: 2 servings | Prep: | Cook: |Ready in: 20mins

Ingredients

- 3 ounces dried apricots
- ¾ cup water
- 1 tablespoon sugar
- 1 2-inch piece vanilla bean, split lengthwise
- 3 tablespoons fresh lemon juice
- ½ cup heavy cream
- 1 tablespoon amaretto liqueur (optional)
- ¼ cup amaretti cookies, coarsely ground

Direction

- Combine apricots, water, sugar, vanilla bean and lemon juice in a 1 1/2-quart souffle dish. Cover tightly with microwave plastic wrap. Cook at 100 percent power in a high-power oven for 8 minutes. Prick plastic to release steam.
- Remove from oven and uncover. Remove the vanilla bean.Transfer mixture to a blender. Cover the blender lid with a kitchen towel and hold down firmly. Blend until smooth. Scrape mixture into a medium bowl. Cool. Refrigerate until cold.
- Whip cream until soft peaks form. Add amaretto (optional). Whip until cream holds firmer but not stiff peaks. Stir a third of the cream into the apricot puree. Fold in the remaining cream. Divide mixture between two 1-cup souffle dishes. Cover with plastic wrap. Freeze at least 4 hours or overnight. Let stand at room temperature for 20 minutes before serving. Sprinkle the top of each mousse with ground cookies.

Nutrition Information

- 376: calories;
- 7 grams: monounsaturated fat;
- 3 grams: protein;
- 23 grams: fat;
- 14 grams: saturated fat;
- 1 gram: polyunsaturated fat;
- 42 grams: carbohydrates;
- 33 grams: sugars;
- 60 milligrams: sodium;

87. Gajar Halwa (Glazed Carrot Fudge)

Serving: Six servings | Prep: | Cook: | Ready in: 30mins

Ingredients

- 2 tablespoons sweet butter, plus about 1 tablespoon for greasing the bowl
- 3 cups grated carrots, lightly packed (about 1 pound whole carrots)
- 2 cups light cream or half-and-half
- ½ teaspoon red food coloring (optional)
- ¼ cup sugar
- 1 teaspoon ground cardamom
- ½ cup raisins
- 2 tablespoons chopped pistachio nuts
- ½ cup slivered almonds

Direction

- Butter a shallow 1 1/2-cup bowl and set aside. In a 2 1/2-quart microwave-proof dish, combine the carrots, cream and coloring, if desired. Cook, uncovered, at 100 percent power in a 650- to 700-watt microwave carousel oven for 25 minutes, or until the cream reduces to a thick sauce and coats the carrot shreds. Stir 3 times during the cooking time.
- Remove from the oven, add the remaining 2 tablespoons of butter, the sugar, cardamom, raisins, pistachios and 1/4 cup of the almonds.

Mix well. Cook, uncovered, at 100 percent power for 5 to 7 minutes, or until the mixture is the consistency of tapioca pudding and there is no longer any bubbling liquid. Stir once during the cooking time. Remove from the oven.

- Transfer the fudge into the buttered bowl and pack it in evenly. Place a serving plate upside down over the bowl. Holding both the plate and bowl securely, invert the bowl over the plate so that the fudge slides onto the plate. Decorate the fudge with the remaining almonds and serve.

Nutrition Information

- 463: calories;
- 22 grams: sugars;
- 20 grams: saturated fat;
- 4 grams: dietary fiber;
- 3 grams: polyunsaturated fat;
- 31 grams: carbohydrates;
- 6 grams: protein;
- 82 milligrams: sodium;
- 37 grams: fat;
- 0 grams: trans fat;
- 13 grams: monounsaturated fat;

88. Gefilte Fish

Serving: 8 servings | Prep: | Cook: | Ready in: 1hours30mins

Ingredients

- To make the fish stock:
- 3 pounds fish heads, skin and bones, rinsed, well and gills removed, cut in small pieces
- 1 medium-size carrot, trimmed, peeled and quartered
- 1 medium-size onion, peeled and quartered
- ½ rib of celery, peeled and quartered
- 1 bay leaf
- 4 cups water

- 1 ½ tablespoons kosher salt
- 3 medium-size carrots, trimmed, peeled and sliced crosswise 1/8-inch thick
- To make the fish mixture
- ¼ pound white fish fillets, skinned
- ¼ pound carp fillets, skinned
- ¼ pound pike fillets, skinned
- 1 medium-size onion, peeled and quartered
- 2 large eggs
- 6 tablespoons matzoh meal
- 6 tablespoons cold water
- ½ teaspoon kosher salt
- Pinch freshly ground black pepper
- ½ to 1 teaspoon unflavored gelatin, as needed
- Red and white horseradish

Direction

- To make the stock, place all the ingredients for the stock except the carrot slices in a two-quart souffle dish. Cover tightly with microwave plastic wrap. Cook at 100 percent power in a high-power oven for 30 minutes. Prick plastic.
- Remove from oven. Uncover and strain. Pour half of the stock back into dish. Set remaining broth aside. Add sliced carrots to the cooking dish. Cook, covered, for 10 minutes. Prick plastic to release steam.
- Remove from oven and uncover. Set aside.
- To make the fish mixture, place the fillets and onion in a food processor. Process until smooth. Add the remaining ingredients except gelatin and horseradish and process just until combined. Refrigerate until cold. With damp hands, shape mixture into eight plump ovals, about 1/4 cup each.
- Arrange the ovals in spoke fashion around the edge of a 14-by-11-by-2-inch oval dish. Remove carrots from broth with a slotted spoon and place in center of dish. Pour broth from the dish over all. Cover tightly with microwave plastic wrap, leaving a small vent in one corner. Cook for 10 minutes. Prick plastic.
- Place a small plate in the freezer (to use later to test gel of stock).
- Remove fish from oven. Uncover, and turn each piece over. Let fish cool in the broth for 30 minutes.
- Test the jelly by pouring a spoonful of broth onto the cold plate. Place the plate in the freezer for 1 minute. Broth should be firm. If it is not, place the reserved broth in a bowl and sprinkle 1/2 teaspoon gelatin on top. Let stand for 2 minutes. Stir well and repeat test with chilled plate. If broth is still not firm, add another 1/2 teaspoon gelatin and repeat test.
- Place gefilte fish in the smallest deep container that can hold it in one layer. Cover with all of the broth. Chill fish and broth at least 24 hours.
- Serve gefilte fish chilled, with some of the jelled broth and carrots. Pass horseradish in a separate bowl.

Nutrition Information

- 261: calories;
- 0 grams: trans fat;
- 8 grams: carbohydrates;
- 972 milligrams: sodium;
- 5 grams: fat;
- 2 grams: monounsaturated fat;
- 1 gram: dietary fiber;
- 3 grams: sugars;
- 45 grams: protein;

89. Glazed Orange Rind

Serving: 3 cups glazed rind | Prep: | Cook: | Ready in: 38mins

Ingredients

- Peel from 4 blood oranges, in quarters, with strings removed and cut lengthwise into 1/4-inch-wide strips
- 4 ½ cups cold water
- 4 ounces granulated sugar
- ½ cup raw (turbinado) sugar

Direction

- Place orange rind and 1 1/2 cups of the water in a 2 1/2-quart souffle dish. Cover tightly with microwave plastic wrap and cook at 100 percent power in a 650- to 700-watt oven for 5 minutes. Prick plastic to release steam.
- Remove from oven and uncover. Strain orange peel, discard liquid and return peel to souffle dish with 1 cup cold water. Cover tightly with microwave plastic wrap and cook at 100 percent power for 5 minutes. Repeat this process twice, using half the remaining cold water each time.
- Return drained orange peel to souffle dish and stir in granulated sugar. Cover tightly with microwave plastic wrap and cook at 100 percent power for 8 minutes, stirring once. Prick plastic to release steam.
- Remove from oven and uncover. Place a wire rack over a piece of parchment or wax paper. Put orange slices on the rack so that they do not touch one another. Allow to stand for about 1 hour to dry out slightly.
- Toss orange peel in the raw sugar in a shallow bowl to coat evenly. Return peel to the wire rack to dry out completely, for about 2 hours. Store in an airtight box.

90. Goulash Soup

Serving: 8 to 10 servings | Prep: | Cook: |Ready in: 45mins

Ingredients

- 2 tablespoons medium (sweet-hot) paprika, or mild with 1/4 teaspoon cayenne pepper added
- 1 tablespoon vegetable oil
- 1 medium-size onion, peeled and coarsely chopped (about 1 cup)
- 1 medium-size red bell pepper, cored, seeded and cut into 1/4-inch dice (about 1 cup)
- 3 ½ cups rich meat broth (see recipe)
- 2 ½ pounds beef chuck steak, cut into 1/4-inch cubes
- 2 cloves garlic, smashed, peeled and chopped
- 1 pound potatoes, peeled and cut into 1/4-inch cubes
- ¼ teaspoon caraway seeds
- ½ cup tomato puree
- 1 teaspoon kosher salt, optional

Direction

- Combine paprika and oil in a 5-quart casserole with tight-fitting lid. Form into a mound in the center of the dish. Cook, uncovered, at 100 percent power in a 650- to 700-watt oven for 2 minutes.
- Add onions and peppers and stir to coat with the oil and paprika mixture. Cook, uncovered, at 100 percent power for 3 minutes.
- Remove from oven and stir in 1 cup of the broth with all remaining ingredients except salt. Cover and cook at 100 percent power for 15 minutes.
- Remove from oven and uncover. Stir in remaining broth, re-cover and cook at 100 percent power for 10 minutes.
- Remove from oven and stir in salt, if desired. Serve over noodles.

Nutrition Information

- 323: calories;
- 21 grams: fat;
- 1 gram: trans fat;
- 10 grams: monounsaturated fat;
- 114 milligrams: sodium;
- 8 grams: saturated fat;
- 2 grams: sugars;
- 12 grams: carbohydrates;
- 23 grams: protein;

91. Greek Stuffed Grape Leaves

Serving: 45 to 50 stuffed leaves | Prep: | Cook: |Ready in: 1hours30mins

Ingredients

- 1 jar grape leaves in brine, or 45 to 50 fresh leaves soaked in brine
- ¼ cup plus 2 tablespoons olive oil
- ¼ cup finely chopped onion
- 1 large clove garlic, peeled, smashed and chopped fine
- ½ cup long-grain rice
- 1 ½ teaspoons dried mint
- 2 cups water
- ¾ cup lemon juice

Direction

- Drain grape leaves and rinse very well under cold running water. Allow to soak in fresh water for at least 1 hour.
- Place 2 tablespoons of the olive oil in an 8-by-8 by 2-inch glass or ceramic dish. Cook, uncovered, at 100 percent power in a high-power oven for 2 minutes. Stir in onion and garlic. Cook, uncovered, for 2 minutes.
- Stir in rice, mint and 1 cup of the water. Cover tightly with microwave plastic wrap. Cook for 10 minutes. Prick plastic to release steam.
- Remove from oven and uncover. Allow to cool slightly.
- Place one grape leaf outside down on work surface. Remove stem with a small knife. Place 1 rounded teaspoon of the rice mixture in the center of the leaf. Fold the sides to the center and roll up. Place, seam side down in an 11-by-7 by 2 1/2-inch glass dish. Repeat with remaining rice mixture and leaves.
- Pour remaining water and 1/2 cup of the lemon juice over the grape leaves. Cover and cook for 18 minutes. Prick plastic to release steam.
- Remove from oven and uncover. Allow to stand until cool. Pour over remaining 1/4 cup olive oil and remaining 1/4 cup lemon juice. Cover and refrigerate for at least 6 hours.

Nutrition Information

- 33: calories;
- 2 grams: fat;
- 0 grams: polyunsaturated fat;
- 1 gram: protein;
- 4 grams: carbohydrates;
- 2 milligrams: sodium;

92. Green Potage

Serving: Five and a half cups | Prep: | Cook: |Ready in: 25mins

Ingredients

- 1 tablespoon unsalted butter
- 1 medium onion (6 ounces) peeled, halved and thinly sliced
- 1 pound potatoes, peeled and cut into 1-inch pieces
- 3 ½ cups chicken broth, homemade or canned
- ½ pound broccoli, stemmed, peeled and cut into coins and florets
- ½ pound spinach, stemmed and washed
- 1 teaspoon kosher salt, or to taste
- Freshly ground black pepper to taste

Direction

- Place the butter in an oval dish measuring 13 by 9 by 2 inches. Cook, uncovered, in a 650- to 700-watt microwave oven at 100 percent power for 1 minute. Add the onions and stir to coat. Cook, uncovered, at 100 percent power for 3 minutes.
- Add the potatoes around the inside edge of the dish. Pour 1/2 cup of the broth over the potatoes. Cover tightly with microwave plastic wrap. Cook at 100 percent power for 4 minutes. Prick the plastic to release steam.
- Remove from the oven and uncover. Place the broccoli in a ring inside the potatoes and spread the spinach over all. Cover tightly with

microwave plastic wrap and cook at 100 percent power for 10 minutes. Prick the plastic to release steam.

- Remove from the oven and uncover. Pass the mixture through the medium blade of a food mill into a large saucepan, gradually adding the remaining broth. Stir in salt and pepper and place over moderate heat until hot.

Nutrition Information

- 160: calories;
- 0 grams: polyunsaturated fat;
- 1 gram: monounsaturated fat;
- 25 grams: carbohydrates;
- 8 grams: protein;
- 4 grams: dietary fiber;
- 2 grams: saturated fat;
- 5 grams: sugars;
- 562 milligrams: sodium;

93. Grilled Tuna And Fennel With Lemon Mint Vinaigrette

Serving: 4 servings | Prep: | Cook: | Ready in: 30mins

Ingredients

- ½ cup extra-virgin olive oil
- ½ cup fresh lemon juice
- 3 tablespoons soy sauce
- 1 teaspoon kosher salt
- 3 small bulbs fennel, quartered
- 4 7- to 8-ounce tuna steaks, each about 1 1/4 inches thick
- ¼ cup chopped mint
- 2 tablespoons chopped chives
- 2 tablespoons chopped parsley
- 2 teaspoons chopped tarragon

Direction

- Preheat a charcoal grill or a broiler. In a small bowl, whisk together the oil, lemon juice, soy sauce and salt. Set aside.
- Place the fennel in a large microwave-safe bowl, cover with plastic wrap and microwave on high until the fennel just begins to become tender, about 6 to 7 minutes. Drain the fennel and brush it lightly with the oil-and-lemon mixture. Grill or broil until lightly browned and very tender, about 8 to 10 minutes.
- Meanwhile, brush the tuna with some of the oil-and-lemon mixture and grill or broil until seared but red in the center, 2 to 3 minutes per side. Transfer to a platter and surround with the fennel. Combine the herbs with the remaining oil-and-lemon mixture and pour it over the tuna. Serve immediately.

Nutrition Information

- 529: calories;
- 55 grams: protein;
- 984 milligrams: sodium;
- 4 grams: saturated fat;
- 3 grams: polyunsaturated fat;
- 13 grams: carbohydrates;
- 5 grams: dietary fiber;
- 29 grams: fat;
- 0 grams: trans fat;
- 20 grams: monounsaturated fat;
- 6 grams: sugars;

94. Ham And Pineapple Curry

Serving: Four to six servings | Prep: | Cook: | Ready in: 20mins

Ingredients

- 1 large onion, peeled and cut into 1/2-inch dice, about 1 cup
- 2 medium green bell peppers, seeded, deribbed and cut into 1/2-inch dice, about 1 1/2 cups

- 4 garlic cloves, minced
- 1 tablespoon vegetable oil
- 1 tablespoon curry powder
- 1 teaspoon black mustard seeds
- 1 tablespoon cornstarch
- ½ cup apple juice or canned pineapple juice
- 1 tablespoon lemon juice
- 1 ½ pounds baked ham, cut into 3/4-inch chunks
- 12 ounces fresh pineapple, peeled and cored (or canned in juice, unsweetened), cut into 1-inch chunks (about 2 cups)
- ½ cup chopped coriander (optional)

Direction

- Combine the onion, peppers, garlic, oil, curry powder and mustard seeds in a two-and-one-half-quart souffle dish or casserole. Cover tightly with microwave-safe plastic wrap. Cook at 100 percent power in a 650- to 700-watt oven for eight minutes, stirring once halfway through the cooking time. Prick the plastic to release the steam.
- Remove from the oven and uncover. In a small bowl, combine the cornstarch, apple or pineapple juice and lemon juice. Stir into the vegetables and spices. Add the ham and pineapple chunks. Cover with microwave-safe plastic wrap. Cook at 100 percent power for seven minutes. Prick the plastic to release the steam.
- Remove from the oven and uncover. Stir in the coriander, if desired, and serve.

Nutrition Information

- 275: calories;
- 4 grams: dietary fiber;
- 0 grams: trans fat;
- 7 grams: monounsaturated fat;
- 13 grams: fat;
- 1 gram: polyunsaturated fat;
- 21 grams: carbohydrates;
- 10 grams: sugars;
- 20 grams: protein;

- 1301 milligrams: sodium;

95. Haydee's Microwave Bananas

Serving: 4 servings | Prep: | Cook: | Ready in: 2mins

Ingredients

- 2 very ripe soft bananas, peeled and sliced lengthwise
- 2 tablespoons unsalted butter
- 2 heaping tablespoons brown sugar
- ¼ teaspoon cinnamon

Direction

- Place bananas in a ceramic bowl with all other ingredients. Do not mix. Microwave on high for 1 to 2 minutes. Spoon on top of pancakes.

Nutrition Information

- 120: calories;
- 18 grams: carbohydrates;
- 11 grams: sugars;
- 1 gram: protein;
- 6 grams: fat;
- 4 grams: saturated fat;
- 0 grams: polyunsaturated fat;
- 2 grams: dietary fiber;
- 3 milligrams: sodium;

96. Hot And Sour Soba Salad

Serving: Serves six | Prep: | Cook: | Ready in: 15mins

Ingredients

- 1 to 2 tablespoons peanut butter (to taste)
- 1 tablespoon soy sauce
- 2 tablespoons white wine vinegar or seasoned rice wine vinegar

- 1 to 2 teaspoons hot red pepper oil (to taste)
- Pinch of cayenne
- 1 large garlic clove, minced
- 2 teaspoons finely minced fresh ginger
- Salt
- freshly ground pepper to taste
- 1 tablespoon sesame oil
- 2 tablespoons canola oil
- ½ cup vegetable or chicken broth
- ½ pound Japanese buckwheat noodles
- 1 cup diced or julienned cucumber
- ¼ cup chopped cilantro
- ¼ cup coarsely chopped walnuts
- Lettuce, baby spinach, radicchio or arugula for serving (optional)

Direction

- Heat the peanut butter for 10 to 20 seconds in a microwave to make it easier to mix. Combine with the soy sauce, vinegar, hot red pepper oil, cayenne, garlic, ginger and salt and pepper. Whisk together. Whisk in the sesame oil, canola oil and broth. Set aside.
- To cook the noodles, bring a large pot of water to a boil, and add salt, if desired, and the noodles. When the water comes back to a boil and bubbles up, add a cup of cold water to the pot. Allow the water to come back to a boil, and add another cup of cold water. Allow the water to come to a boil one more time, and add a third cup of water. When the water comes to a boil again, the noodles should be cooked through. Drain and toss immediately with the dressing (whisk the dressing again first). Add the remaining ingredients, and toss together. Taste, adjust seasonings, and serve over a bed of salad greens if desired.

Nutrition Information

- 269: calories;
- 1 gram: sugars;
- 476 milligrams: sodium;
- 14 grams: fat;
- 2 grams: saturated fat;

- 0 grams: trans fat;
- 6 grams: polyunsaturated fat;
- 32 grams: carbohydrates;
- 8 grams: protein;

97. Irish Stew

Serving: 6 to 8 servings (makes 8 cups; 362 calories per cup) | Prep: | Cook: |Ready in: 45mins

Ingredients

- 2 pounds stewing lamb (neck or shoulder) with bones, cut into 1- or 2-inch chunks
- 3 medium-size carrots, scraped and cut into pieces about 2 by 1/4 by 1/4 inches
- ½ pound small white onions, peeled
- 1 pound small new potatoes, or 1 pound large potatoes cut in half or quartered
- ½ pound small turnips, scrubbed and cut into 8 wedges each
- 1 tablespoon kosher salt
- Freshly ground black pepper to taste
- 1 ½ cups water
- 1 cup peas (if they are frozen, place in a sieve under warm running water to defrost)
- ½ cup chopped fresh mint

Direction

- Place lamb in two layers around inside rim of an oval dish, about 10 by 8 by 3 inches. Mound carrots, onions, potatoes and turnips in center. Sprinkle with salt and pepper. Add water. Cover tightly with microwave plastic wrap. Cook at 100 percent power for 20 minutes.
- Remove from oven. Prick plastic with the tip of a sharp knife to release steam. Uncover dish carefully. Stir well, making sure any uncooked pieces of meat are on top. Stir in peas. Recover dish with a fresh piece of plastic. Cook at 100 percent power for 5 minutes.
- Remove from oven. Prick plastic and remove. Stir in mint and serve immediately, or allow stew to mellow overnight and add mint after

reheating from room temperature for 5 minutes. If you are reheating from the refrigerator, it will take 10 minutes.

Nutrition Information

- 412: calories;
- 5 grams: sugars;
- 27 grams: fat;
- 12 grams: saturated fat;
- 20 grams: carbohydrates;
- 742 milligrams: sodium;
- 11 grams: monounsaturated fat;
- 2 grams: polyunsaturated fat;
- 4 grams: dietary fiber;
- 22 grams: protein;

98. Jellied Fish Broth

Serving: 5 cups | Prep: | Cook: | Ready in: 58mins

Ingredients

- 2 ¼ pounds fish bones and heads, well cleaned of blood and cut into pieces 2 to 3 inches in length
- 5 cups cold water
- Large pinch thread saffron
- ⅓ cup white wine
- 2 ounces canned tomatoes (in juice)
- 2 tablespoons tomato paste
- 7 cloves garlic, peeled and smashed
- ½ teaspoon ground fennel
- ½ teaspoon kosher salt

Direction

- Combine the fish bones and water in a 5-quart glass or ceramic casserole. Cover tightly with microwave plastic wrap. Cook at 100 percent power in a 650- to 700-watt oven for 40 minutes.
- Remove the broth from the oven. Prick the plastic with a sharp knife to release steam.

Uncover carefully and let stand until cool. Strain through a fine sieve lined with a kitchen towel or cheesecloth rung out in cold water. Reserve the broth. Rinse and dry the casserole.

- Combine saffron and wine in the clean casserole. Cook, uncovered, at 100 percent power for 30 seconds.
- Place the tomatoes, tomato paste, garlic and 1/4 cup of the reserved stock in a blender. Blend until smooth. Add to the saffron-wine mixture. Stir in fennel, salt and remaining broth. Cover tightly with microwave plastic wrap. Cook at 100 percent power for 8 minutes.
- Remove from oven. Prick the plastic to release steam. Uncover and transfer soup to a serving bowl or individual bowls. Chill in the refrigerator overnight or until jelled.

Nutrition Information

- 44: calories;
- 2 grams: fat;
- 0 grams: sugars;
- 7 grams: protein;
- 168 milligrams: sodium;

99. Light Mushroom Soup

Serving: 4 cups | Prep: | Cook: | Ready in: 16mins

Ingredients

- 1 ½ tablespoons unsalted butter
- ½ pound fresh mushrooms, quartered
- 1 scallion, thinly sliced, equal parts green and white
- 1 tablespoon finely chopped celery leaves (optional)
- 1 tablespoon cornstarch
- 2 cups chicken broth
- 1 cup heavy cream
- ½ teaspoon ground cumin
- Pinch dill seed

- 1 tablespoon dried boletus, crumbled (optional)
- 2 teaspoons coarse kosher salt
- 2 teaspoons fresh lemon juice
- 4 drops hot pepper sauce

Direction

- In a 2 1/2-quart souffle dish, melt butter, uncovered at 100 percent power for 1 minute 15 seconds. Meanwhile, finely chop mushrooms in food processor. Add to melted butter, with scallions and celery leaves. Stir to coat with butter. Cook, uncovered, at 100 percent power for 3 minutes or until mushrooms look limp.
- Dissolve cornstarch in chicken broth. Add chicken broth mixture, cream, cumin, dill seed and dried boletus, if used, to mushrooms. Cover tightly with polyvinyl plastic wrap. Cook at 100 percent power for 6 minutes. Pierce plastic to release steam. Season with salt, lemon juice and hot pepper sauce. Serve hot.

Nutrition Information

- 206: calories;
- 19 grams: fat;
- 1 gram: polyunsaturated fat;
- 3 grams: sugars;
- 4 grams: protein;
- 11 grams: saturated fat;
- 0 grams: dietary fiber;
- 5 grams: monounsaturated fat;
- 7 grams: carbohydrates;
- 388 milligrams: sodium;

100.   Light Vichyssoise

Serving: 4 cups | Prep: | Cook: | Ready in: 15mins

Ingredients

- ¾ pounds potatoes, peeled and coarsely chopped in a food processor
- 2 leeks (1/2 pound each) dark green end discarded, cleaned and coarsely chopped in the food processor
- 2 ¼ cups chicken broth
- ⅓ cup part skim-milk ricotta cheese
- ½ cup buttermilk
- ½ teaspoon kosher salt
- 2 tablespoons chopped fresh chives, optional

Direction

- Place the potatoes and leeks in a 2-quart souffle dish and add 1 1/2 cups of the broth. Cover tightly with microwave plastic. Cook in a 650- to 700-watt oven at 100 percent power for 10 minutes.
- While the potatoes and leeks are cooking, combine the ricotta and 1/4 cup of the broth in the food processor. Process until very smooth.
- Remove potato and leek mixture from oven. Prick the plastic to release steam and uncover. Add to the food processor with the remaining broth and process until very smooth. Remove to a serving bowl. Stir in the buttermilk and salt and chill for 3 hours or overnight. Serve with a sprinkling of chives on top, if desired.

Nutrition Information

- 193: calories;
- 5 grams: fat;
- 2 grams: monounsaturated fat;
- 29 grams: carbohydrates;
- 9 grams: protein;
- 0 grams: polyunsaturated fat;
- 3 grams: dietary fiber;
- 6 grams: sugars;
- 519 milligrams: sodium;

101. Liz Schillinger's Shenandoah Berry Pie

Serving: Serves 8 | Prep: | Cook: | Ready in: 5hours30mins

Ingredients

- For the dough:
- 2 cups unbleached all-purpose flour, plus more for rolling out the dough
- 1 teaspoon salt
- ½ pound (1 cup) lard
- For the filling:
- 1 cup sugar
- ¼ cup unbleached all-purpose flour
- ½ teaspoon freshly grated lemon zest
- ¼ teaspoon salt
- 5 cups blueberries and sliced strawberries (any mixture you like)
- 2 teaspoons fresh lemon juice
- 1 tablespoon melted unsalted butter

Direction

- Place a marble pastry slab and marble rolling pin in the freezer until very cold, at least 4 hours.
- To make the pie dough, in a medium bowl, whisk the flour and salt together. Place the lard in a glass measuring cup and microwave on high until almost but not completely melted, about 1 minute. Remove from microwave and stir until completely melted. Pour into 1-cup measuring cup and then remove 2 tablespoons of the lard. Add 2 tablespoons of water and mix; you should have exactly 1 cup liquid. Stir liquid into flour with a wooden spoon for a few seconds until the dough holds together.
- Remove the slab and pin from freezer. Flour the slab lightly. Place a cloth cover on the marble rolling pin and flour lightly. Working quickly, roll the dough out to a thickness of between 1/8 and 1 1/816 inch. If the dough is sticky and doesn't roll smoothly, it may be too warm; pop the whole thing (slab and dough)

back in the freezer for a few minutes to chill it before working it again. If the dough is too stiff and begins to crack and shatter, it is too cold; walk away for a few minutes and then try working it again. Use your fingers to press together any cracks or fix any holes in the dough.

- Invert a 9-inch pie plate onto one side of the dough. Using a paring knife, cut a circle around it, making the circle 1/2 inch larger in diameter than the plate. Using 2 spatulas, loosen the dough from the slab; it should be very stiff and come up easily in one piece. (If it sags or sticks, pop the whole thing back in the freezer for a few minutes.) Lift the dough with the spatulas and center it over the pie plate. Let it sit on the plate until it warms up and sags into the plate. (Don't worry if it has some cracks.) Press the edges in gently with your fingers and fix any tears by pressing the dough together. Crimp the edges.
- Cut small basset-hound shapes, or any decorations you like, from the remaining dough. Set aside.
- Preheat the oven to 375 degrees. To make the filling, in a large bowl whisk together the sugar, flour, zest and salt. Add the fruit and toss to combine. Add the lemon juice and butter and toss again. Scrape into the prepared crust and lay your decorations over the top. Bake until the crust is browned and the fruit is bubbling, about 1 hour. Remove from oven and let cool.

Nutrition Information

- 579: calories;
- 12 grams: saturated fat;
- 0 grams: trans fat;
- 13 grams: monounsaturated fat;
- 31 grams: fat;
- 4 grams: polyunsaturated fat;
- 73 grams: carbohydrates;
- 5 grams: protein;
- 39 grams: sugars;
- 366 milligrams: sodium;

102. Masala Vangi (Eggplant Slices Smothered With Coconut Spice Paste)

Serving: Four servings | Prep: | Cook: |Ready in: 30mins

Ingredients

- 2 tablespoons yellow split peas
- 2 tablespoons coriander seeds
- 2 teaspoons cumin seeds
- ½ cup coconut flakes, sweetened or unsweetened
- ¼ to ½ teaspoon cayenne
- ¼ teaspoon dried thyme
- 3 tablespoons light sesame or peanut oil
- 1 teaspoon mustard seeds
- 4 medium-size cloves garlic, peeled and sliced thin
- ½ cup chopped onion
- 1 tablespoon lemon juice
- 1 medium-size eggplant (about 1 pound), stemmed, halved and cut lengthwise into 1/2-inch-thick slices
- 2 teaspoons coarse salt, or to taste
- Grated coconut for garnish (optional)
- Lemon juice for garnish (optional)
- Fresh chopped cilantro for garnish (optional)

Direction

- Combine the peas, coriander and cumin in a spice mill or coffee grinder and grind to a fine powder. Transfer the pea-spice mixture to a small bowl and set aside.
- Place the coconut, cayenne, thyme and 2/3 cup of water in the bowl of a blender or food processor and process to a fine puree. Transfer the coconut-spice mixture to a separate bowl and set aside.
- Place a 10-inch microwave-proof covered shallow dish in a 650- to 700-watt microwave carousel oven, add the oil and heat at 100 percent power for 2 minutes. Uncover, add the mustard seeds and replace the lid. Cook at 100 percent power for 2 to 3 minutes, or until the seeds pop. Uncover, stir in the pea-spice mixture and the garlic and onion. Replace the lid and cook at 100 percent power for 4 minutes, or until onions are soft. Remove.
- Add the coconut-spice mixture and lemon juice and mix thoroughly. Cook, uncovered, at 100 percent power for 3 minutes, or until the coconut-spice paste begins to thicken. Remove from the oven.
- Add the eggplant and salt. Mix until the vegetables are evenly coated with the spice paste. Cover and cook at 100 percent power for 6 to 8 minutes, or until the eggplant is cooked soft but not mushy. Remove from the oven and let the dish stand, covered, for 5 minutes. Garnish with the coconut, lemon juice and coriander, if desired, and serve.

Nutrition Information

- 230: calories;
- 18 grams: fat;
- 8 grams: dietary fiber;
- 6 grams: sugars;
- 4 grams: protein;
- 17 grams: carbohydrates;
- 394 milligrams: sodium;

103. Mediterranean Fish Soup

Serving: Six servings | Prep: | Cook: |Ready in: 30mins

Ingredients

- 1 medium onion, peeled and coarsely chopped, about 1 cup
- 5 cloves garlic, smashed, peeled and sliced
- Pinch cayenne pepper
- 1 tablespoon vegetable oil
- 4 cups fish broth (see recipe)

- 1 ½ pounds tomatoes, cored and roughly chopped, about 3 cups
- ½ cup white wine
- ¼ cup Pernod
- Large pinch saffron threads
- 1 tablespoon freshly squeezed lemon juice
- Kosher salt and freshly ground pepper to taste
- Croutons (optional)

Direction

- Combine the onion, garlic, cayenne pepper and oil in a five-quart casserole with a tightly fitting lid. Cover and cook at 100 percent power in a 650- to 700-watt oven for four minutes.
- Remove and uncover. Stir in the broth, tomatoes, wine, Pernod and saffron. Cover and cook at 100 percent power for 15 minutes.
- Remove and uncover. Pass through a food mill with a medium blade. Stir in the lemon juice and season with salt and pepper.
- Serve hot with croutons, if desired.

Nutrition Information

- 118: calories;
- 2 grams: dietary fiber;
- 1 gram: polyunsaturated fat;
- 9 grams: carbohydrates;
- 5 grams: protein;
- 769 milligrams: sodium;
- 4 grams: sugars;
- 0 grams: trans fat;

104.   Microwave Mixed Rice

Serving: 1 serving | Prep: | Cook: | Ready in: 10mins

Ingredients

- 1 ½ cups cooked rice
- 1 cup (more or less) leftover cooked vegetables or meat

- ¼ cup vinaigrette, sesame dipping sauce, tahini sauce, pico de gallo, onion chutney, pesto, hummus or any other sauce you like
- Salt and ground black pepper

Direction

- Toss ingredients in a large bowl, stir to combine and season with salt and pepper. Microwave for 1 minute.
- Stir and cook for another minute or 2 or until warm. Serve.

Nutrition Information

- 478: calories;
- 89 grams: carbohydrates;
- 9 grams: dietary fiber;
- 0 grams: sugars;
- 7 grams: fat;
- 1 gram: saturated fat;
- 3 grams: polyunsaturated fat;
- 14 grams: protein;
- 908 milligrams: sodium;

105.   Microwave Nut Brittle

Serving: About 2 pounds | Prep: | Cook: | Ready in: 40mins

Ingredients

- 2 cups raw nuts or seeds
- 2 cups sugar
- 1 cup corn syrup
- ½ teaspoon salt
- 2 tablespoons butter
- 1 teaspoon baking soda
- 1 teaspoon vanilla extract

Direction

- Chop the nuts or seeds if they are large; otherwise, leave them whole. Put them into a 4-quart glass bowl with all other ingredients except the baking soda and vanilla extract. Stir in 3/4 cup water. Heat in a microwave oven on high power for 5 minutes. Using oven mitts or potholders, carefully transfer the bowl to a countertop and stir with a heat-resistant spatula. Repeat 2 or 3 more times, until the syrup thickens and the nuts begin to stick together. Then heat for 1-minute periods, stirring in between, until the syrup begins to turn light golden brown.

- Line a baking sheet with foil. Add the baking soda and vanilla extract to the syrup and stir vigorously. Quickly pour the mixture out onto the baking sheet and use the spatula to spread it as thin as possible. Allow to cool to room temperature, then peel off the foil and break the brittle into pieces. Store in an airtight container.

Nutrition Information

- 311: calories;
- 175 milligrams: sodium;
- 2 grams: dietary fiber;
- 0 grams: trans fat;
- 52 grams: carbohydrates;
- 12 grams: fat;
- 7 grams: monounsaturated fat;
- 47 grams: sugars;
- 3 grams: protein;

106.   Microwave Paella

Serving: 8 to 10 servings | Prep: | Cook: | Ready in: 1hours13mins

Ingredients

- 2 medium-size onions, peeled and diced (about 1 1/2 cups)
- 24 cloves garlic, smashed and peeled
- 3 medium-size tomatoes, cored and diced (about 3 cups)
- 1 tablespoon extra-virgin olive oil
- 2 cups white rice
- 2 bay leaves
- 1 tablespoon paprika
- ½ teaspoon dried thyme
- 2 ½ cups homemade chicken broth or unsalted canned broth
- 1 teaspoon saffron threads
- 5 ounces chorizo, cut across into 1/8-inch slices
- 4 ounces pimentos, rinsed under cold water and cut into thin strips
- 12 chicken thighs, about 3 1/2 pounds, skinned and any fat removed
- 12 littleneck clams, scrubbed
- 5 ounces frozen peas, defrosted under warm running water (about 2/3 cup)
- 20 small mussels (or 12 large), scrubbed and debearded
- 18 large shrimp, peeled and deveined
- ¼ cup chopped fresh parsley
- Kosher salt and freshly ground black pepper, to taste

Direction

- Place onions and garlic in the work bowl of a food processor and process until coarsely chopped. Scrape into a 5-quart casserole with tight-fitting lid. Stir in tomatoes and oil. Cook, uncovered, at 100 percent power in a 650- to 700-watt oven for 6 minutes.
- Remove from oven and stir in rice, bay leaves, paprika and thyme. Cook, uncovered, at 100 percent power for 4 minutes.
- Remove from oven and stir in chicken broth and saffron. Cook, uncovered, at 100 percent power for 9 minutes. Stir, then cook, uncovered, for 8 minutes longer.
- Remove from oven, stir in chorizo and scatter pimento strips over. Place chicken pieces over rice mixture in a single layer. Cover dish with lid and cook at 100 percent power for 4 minutes.
- Remove from oven and uncover. With a large spoon, transfer chicken pieces to a plate. Stir rice mixture well. Return chicken pieces to the casserole so that they are turned over. Cook,

- covered, at 100 percent power for 4 minutes longer.
- Remove from oven and uncover. Place clams, hinge end down, around the inside edge of the casserole. Cook, covered, at 100 percent power for 3 minutes.
- Remove from oven and uncover. Move clams to the center of the casserole. Scatter peas over the chicken, place mussels, hinge end down, around the inside edge of the dish and place shrimp over mussels. Re-cover with lid and cook at 100 percent power for 5 minutes.
- Remove from oven and uncover. To serve, place all seafood and chicken in a ring on a large platter. Remove bay leaves, stir parsley into rice and season to taste with salt and pepper. Mound rice in the center of the platter.

Nutrition Information

- 568: calories;
- 0 grams: trans fat;
- 44 grams: carbohydrates;
- 12 grams: monounsaturated fat;
- 5 grams: polyunsaturated fat;
- 2 grams: dietary fiber;
- 4 grams: sugars;
- 34 grams: protein;
- 27 grams: fat;
- 8 grams: saturated fat;
- 984 milligrams: sodium;

107.   Microwave Pralines

Serving: About 30 pralines | Prep: | Cook: | Ready in: 40mins

Ingredients

- 3 cups pecans
- 1 ½ cups granulated sugar
- 1 ½ cups light brown sugar
- ¾ cup heavy cream
- ⅓ cup milk
- ⅓ cup butter
- ¾ teaspoon salt
- 1 teaspoon vanilla extract

Direction

- Spread the pecans on a baking sheet and bake in a 350-degree oven until lightly toasted, 10 to 15 minutes.
- Combine all the ingredients except the pecans and vanilla extract in a 4-quart glass bowl. Heat in a microwave oven on high power for 5 minutes. Using oven mitts or potholders, carefully transfer the bowl to a countertop and stir with a heat-resistant spatula. Return to microwave and heat for 5 more minutes.
- Stir in the pecans and heat for another 5 minutes. Stir and check the temperature with a digital or candy thermometer. If it reads 240 degrees, proceed to Step 4. If not, continue heating on high power, stirring and checking the temperature every minute until it does.
- Remove from oven and let the mix sit undisturbed. After 20 minutes, add the vanilla extract and stir vigorously until it becomes cloudy and creamy. Using 2 spoons, scoop and shape into 2-inch-diameter mounds on a baking sheet lined with foil, parchment paper or a silicone mat. If the mix becomes too hard to shape, reheat for 15 seconds. Let the pralines rest for 30 minutes. Keep stored in an airtight container.

Nutrition Information

- 175: calories;
- 11 grams: fat;
- 0 grams: trans fat;
- 5 grams: monounsaturated fat;
- 2 grams: polyunsaturated fat;
- 19 grams: carbohydrates;
- 1 gram: protein;
- 64 milligrams: sodium;
- 3 grams: saturated fat;
- 18 grams: sugars;

108. Microwave Saffron Turkish Delight

Serving: About 120 pieces | Prep: | Cook: | Ready in: 45mins

Ingredients

- 1 ¼ cups cornstarch, plus more for dusting
- 3 cups sugar
- ¼ cup corn syrup
- 1 teaspoon saffron threads
- 2 tablespoons lemon juice
- 1 vanilla bean
- Cooking oil, for greasing pan
- ½ cup powdered sugar

Direction

- Pour 2 1/2 cups water into a 4-quart glass bowl. Slowly whisk in 3/4 cup cornstarch until smooth. Transfer to the microwave and cook on high power for 2 minutes. Using oven mitts or potholders, carefully transfer to a countertop and stir with a heat-resistant spatula. Return to microwave and heat 1 minute at a time, stirring between heatings, until the mixture thickens, bubbles and becomes translucent, about 5 to 6 minutes. Then heat on half power for 3 minutes.
- Mix in the sugar, corn syrup and saffron. Heat on high power for 5 minutes. Stir and repeat, then stir and repeat again. After the last time, stir in the lemon juice. Slit the vanilla bean lengthwise, scrape all the seeds into the mixture and stir to combine. (Save the bean for another use.)
- Continue to heat on high power for 3-minute periods, stirring in between, until a little syrup scraped onto the edge of a cold plate quickly sets to a tacky solid, from 12 to 21 minutes.
- Grease an 8-by-8-inch baking pan with cooking oil and scrape and spread the mix into it. Allow to rest, uncovered, until it is firm enough to handle, several hours or overnight. Dust the top with cornstarch. Invert onto a

small cutting board, using a spatula if needed, and dust the other side with cornstarch. Transfer the board to the freezer for 30 minutes. Cut into 3/4-inch squares with scissors or a knife.
- Combine the remaining 1/2 cup cornstarch and the powdered sugar, and toss the squares in it. Store the candy in this mixture in a wide, shallow container.

Nutrition Information

- 30: calories;
- 7 grams: carbohydrates;
- 6 grams: sugars;
- 1 milligram: sodium;
- 0 grams: protein;

109. Microwaved Black Cod With Scallions And Ginger

Serving: 4 servings | Prep: | Cook: | Ready in: 15mins

Ingredients

- 2 8-ounce black cod fillets, with skin or not (or use halibut, rockfish, trout, black sea bass, pomfret or sole)
- 4 ¼ teaspoons soy sauce
- ¼ teaspoon sesame oil
- 4 1/4-inch-thick round slices of ginger plus 1 tablespoon finely julienned ginger, for garnish
- 5 or 6 scallions, white and green parts separated and julienned
- 1 ½ teaspoons Shaoxing or other white wine
- 3 ½ tablespoons peanut oil

Direction

- Place each fillet in a separate microwave-safe zip-top bag, then place the bags skin (or skinned) side down next to each other on a microwave-safe plate.

- In a small bowl, combine soy sauce and sesame oil; set aside. Divide ginger coins and white part of scallions between the two bags. Pour half the wine (3/4 teaspoon) into each bag. Microwave until fish becomes opaque and flakes easily, 3 1/2 to 5 minutes in an 800-watt oven. (Cooking times will vary depending on the kind of fish used and the power of the oven; for ovens over 800 watts, lower the power level accordingly.)
- Transfer each fillet to a warm serving plate and drizzle each with half of the soy sauce mixture. Garnish with scallion greens and julienned ginger. In a small pan, heat peanut oil until sizzling. Drizzle the hot oil over each fillet and serve immediately.

Nutrition Information

- 284: calories;
- 5 grams: polyunsaturated fat;
- 1 gram: sugars;
- 21 grams: fat;
- 9 grams: monounsaturated fat;
- 414 milligrams: sodium;
- 6 grams: saturated fat;
- 2 grams: carbohydrates;
- 20 grams: protein;

---

110.   Mint Sorbet

Serving: 6 servings | Prep: | Cook: |Ready in: 15mins

Ingredients

- 2 cups sugar
- 2 cups water
- 3 bunches fresh mint (stems on)
- ½ cup fresh lemon juice

Direction

- Stir sugar, water and mint together in a 2 1/2-quart souffle dish. Cook, uncovered, at 100

percent in a high-power oven for 3 minutes. Stir thoroughly, making sure there are no grains on the bottom of the dish. Cover with a lid or microwave plastic wrap. Cook for 6 minutes. Prick plastic, if used, to release steam.
- Remove from oven and uncover. Let cool. Strain through a fine sieve. Refrigerate until cold, several hours or overnight.
- Whisk lemon juice into syrup. Place in an ice-cream machine and freeze according to manufacturer's instructions.

Nutrition Information

- 269: calories;
- 0 grams: polyunsaturated fat;
- 69 grams: carbohydrates;
- 1 gram: protein;
- 67 grams: sugars;
- 9 milligrams: sodium;

---

111.   Minted Pea Soup

Serving: 5 1/2 cups, serves 4 to 5 | Prep: | Cook: |Ready in: 30mins

Ingredients

- 4 cups shelled fresh peas (1 1/2 pounds), or frozen peas, defrosted in a seive under warm running water
- 3 ½ cups vegetarian broth (see Micro Tips) or canned chicken broth
- 5 teaspoons cornstarch
- 20 fresh mint leaves, cut across into chiffonade
- ½ cup buttermilk
- 1 tablespoon kosher salt
- Freshly ground black pepper to taste

Direction

- Combine peas and 1/4 cup broth in a 2 1/2-quart souffle dish or casserole with a lid. Cover tightly with microwave plastic wrap or with lid. Cook at 100 percent power for 12 minutes in a 650- to 700-watt oven. If using frozen peas, eliminate this step and puree peas with broth as below. If using plastic, prick to release steam.

- Remove from oven and uncover. Pass peas through a food mill fitted with a medium-size disc. Scrape mixture back into casserole.
- Dissolve cornstarch in remaining broth and whisk into pea puree. Add mint. Cover and cook for 8 minutes. If using plastic, prick to release steam.
- Remove from oven. Uncover and stir in remaining ingredients. Serve hot or chilled.

Nutrition Information

- 115: calories;
- 7 grams: sugars;
- 8 grams: protein;
- 810 milligrams: sodium;
- 1 gram: fat;
- 0 grams: polyunsaturated fat;
- 20 grams: carbohydrates;
- 5 grams: dietary fiber;

112.   Minted Rice Pilaf

Serving: 5 cups; 8 servings as a side dish | Prep: | Cook: | Ready in: 43mins

Ingredients

- 10 sprigs mint, stems reserved and leaves chopped (about 1/4 cup)
- 1 ½ cups chicken or vegetarian broth
- 1 ½ cups water
- 1 medium-size onion (about 6 ounces), peeled and finely chopped
- 2 tablespoons olive oil
- 1 ½ cups converted white rice, or basmati
- ½ teaspoon kosher salt
- Freshly ground black pepper to taste

Direction

- Place mint stems, chicken broth and water in a 2 1/2-quart souffle dish or casserole with tight-fitting lid. Cook, covered, at 100 percent power in a 650- to 700-watt oven for 10 minutes. If using plastic, prick to release steam.
- Remove from oven and uncover. Strain liquid and allow liquid to cool to room temperature. Reserve.
- Place onion and oil in the 2 1/2-quart souffle dish or casserole. Cover and cook at 100 percent power for 4 minutes.
- Remove from oven and uncover. Stir in rice. Cook, uncovered, at 100 percent power for 1 minute 30 seconds.
- Remove from oven. Stir in reserved liquid. Re-cover and cook at 100 percent power for 10 minutes.
- Remove from oven and uncover. Stir in 2 tablespoons of the chopped mint leaves. Re-cover and cook for 8 minutes longer.
- Remove from oven and uncover. Stir in remaining chopped mint, salt and pepper. Serve hot.

Nutrition Information

- 172: calories;
- 3 grams: protein;
- 0 grams: polyunsaturated fat;
- 31 grams: carbohydrates;
- 128 milligrams: sodium;
- 4 grams: fat;
- 1 gram: sugars;

113.   Mocha Custard

Serving: 4 servings | Prep: | Cook: | Ready in: 12mins

Ingredients

- 1 cup milk
- ¼ cup heavy cream
- 3 large eggs

- ⅓ cup granulated sugar
- 2 teaspoons cocoa powder
- ½ teaspoon powdered instant coffee
- 2 teaspoons Irish cream liqueur

Direction

- Place milk and cream in a 4-cup measure. Cook, uncovered, at 100 percent power in a high-power oven with a carousel for 2 minutes.
- While milk is cooking, whisk together eggs and sugar in a medium bowl. Combine cocoa and coffee in a small bowl.
- Remove milk from oven and pour into egg mixture, whisking constantly. Whisk in Irish Cream.
- Stir a scant tablespoon of the custard mixture into the cocoa and coffee to form a smooth paste. Scrape the cocoa mixture back into the custard and whisk until well combined.
- Pour into 1/2-cup ramekins and skim any foam from the top of each. Place cups, evenly spaced, around the carousel. Cook, uncovered, at 50 percent power for 6 minutes. Custard will still be partly liquid.
- Remove from oven. Let stand, covered with a towel, for 15 minutes. Refrigerate until firm and well chilled.

Nutrition Information

- 219: calories;
- 21 grams: sugars;
- 7 grams: protein;
- 86 milligrams: sodium;
- 6 grams: saturated fat;
- 3 grams: monounsaturated fat;
- 1 gram: polyunsaturated fat;
- 22 grams: carbohydrates;
- 11 grams: fat;
- 0 grams: dietary fiber;

114.   Mocha Truffles

Serving: 80 truffles | Prep: | Cook: | Ready in: 45mins

Ingredients

- 1 cup heavy whipping cream
- 3 tablespoons granulated sugar
- 4 tablespoons unsalted butter, cut in 1/2-inch pieces
- 10 ounces semisweet chocolate (best quality possible), grated
- 3 tablespoons coffee liqueur
- ½ cup unsweetened cocoa powder
- 2 tablespoons confectioners sugar
- 1 ½ teaspoons instant espresso powder

Direction

- Place cream, sugar and butter in a 4-cup glass measure or a one-quart souffle dish. Cook, uncovered, at 100 percent power in a high-power microwave oven for 2 1/2 minutes.
- Remove from oven. Add chocolate and stir until melted and mixture is smooth. Stir in liqueur. Transfer mixture to a metal bowl. Chill until very firm, about an hour.
- Sift cocoa, confectioners sugar and espresso powder onto a sheet of wax paper. Line a baking sheet that will fit in your refrigerator with wax paper. Rinse a 1-inch melon baller or a measuring teaspoon in hot water. Scoop out a truffle, using the tip of a small knife to help release it.
- Drop the truffle into the cocoa mixture. Coat it with the mixture, touching it as little as possible. Transfer to baking sheet. Repeat with remaining chocolate, rinsing melon baller with hot water each time. If chocolate becomes too soft, chill until firm before continuing.
- Chill truffles until firm, about half an hour. Sprinkle with remaining cocoa mixture. Store in layers separated by wax paper, tightly covered and refrigerated.

Nutrition Information

- 38: calories;
- 3 grams: sugars;
- 2 grams: saturated fat;
- 0 grams: protein;
- 1 gram: monounsaturated fat;
- 4 grams: carbohydrates;
- 2 milligrams: sodium;

115. Molded Chocolate Mousse

Serving: 8 servings | Prep: | Cook: | Ready in: 25mins

Ingredients

- 3 ounces semisweet chocolate
- ¾ cup milk
- ¼ cup sugar
- 1 envelope plain gelatin (1/4 ounce)
- 1 ½ cups heavy cream

Direction

- Melt chocolate (see Micro Tip). Set aside to cool.
- Place milk in a 1-quart souffle dish. Stir in sugar. Sprinkle gelatin on top of milk. Let stand for 1 minute.
- Cook, uncovered, at 100 percent power in a high-power oven for 2 minutes. Whisk. Cook for 1 minute 30 seconds.
- Remove from oven. Pour mixture into bowl for an electric mixer. Place bowl inside another bowl with ice water. Whisk gently but constantly until mixture thickens, about 4 minutes. Remove from ice water.
- Whip milk mixture with an electric mixer on high speed until very thick and fluffy, stopping twice to scrape sides of bowl. With mixer running, gradually pour in cream. Continue to whip on high speed, stopping to scrape sides of bowl, until mixture will hold a soft peak, about 5 minutes.
- With mixer on low speed, pour in chocolate, making sure chocolate falls into the cream

mixture, rather than hitting the side of the bowl. Mix just until incorporated.
- Rinse a 4-cup mold with ice water. Scrape the mixture into the mold. Cover and refrigerate until set, several hours or overnight.
- To unmold, briefly dip mold once or twice into a bowl of hot water. Invert onto serving plate.

Nutrition Information

- 246: calories;
- 20 grams: fat;
- 6 grams: monounsaturated fat;
- 1 gram: dietary fiber;
- 15 grams: carbohydrates;
- 14 grams: sugars;
- 13 grams: saturated fat;
- 3 grams: protein;
- 30 milligrams: sodium;

116. Morning Couscous With Oranges And Dates

Serving: 4 to 6 servings | Prep: | Cook: | Ready in: 1hours

Ingredients

- 1 ½ cups water
- 2 to 3 tablespoons brown sugar or honey (to taste)
- 1 teaspoon orange flower water (optional; available at Middle Eastern markets)
- 3 tablespoons chopped dried apricots
- 2 tablespoons currants or raisins
- 1 tablespoon unsalted butter (optional)
- 1 cup couscous
- ¼ to ½ teaspoon cinnamon, to taste
- ¼ teaspoon salt (optional)
- 2 navel oranges
- 6 dates, pitted and cut in quarters lengthwise
- Pomegranate seeds for garnish

Direction

- Combine the water and brown sugar or honey in a saucepan, and bring to a boil. Turn the heat to medium, and boil gently until the sugar has dissolved. Stir in the optional orange flower water, the chopped apricots and the raisins or currants, and set aside for five minutes.
- Place the couscous in a 2-quart bowl, and add the cinnamon and salt. Stir together. Pour on the hot syrup. Mix together with a fork, spatula or wooden spoon, and set aside for 20 minutes, stirring occasionally. At this point, if not eating right away, cover and refrigerate.
- Shortly before serving, steam the couscous in one of two ways. Line a strainer with a double layer of cheesecloth, and dump the couscous into the strainer. Then set above a pot with 1 inch of boiling water. Cover and steam for 15 minutes, making sure that the water is well below the couscous. Transfer to a bowl, add the butter, and toss together until the butter melts. Alternatively, place the couscous in a microwave and cover tightly with plastic wrap. Microwave for two minutes. Carefully uncover, stir in the butter and cover again. Microwave for another two minutes. Remove the plastic, being careful of the steam in the bowl.
- With a paring knife, peel away the skin and pith from the orange, holding it over the couscous so that any juice drips onto the couscous. Still holding the orange over the couscous, cut out the sections from between the membranes.
- Pile the couscous into a mound on a platter, or spoon into individual serving bowls. Decorate with orange sections, date slices and pomegranate seeds, and serve.

Nutrition Information

- 231: calories;
- 55 grams: carbohydrates;
- 5 grams: protein;
- 28 grams: sugars;
- 8 milligrams: sodium;

- 0 grams: polyunsaturated fat;

---

117. Morning Oatmeal With Cherries And Pistachios

Serving: Two servings | Prep: | Cook: | Ready in: 15mins

Ingredients

- ½ cup steel-cut oatmeal, preferably the quick-cooking variety
- Salt to taste
- 1 ½ cups water
- 1 to 2 teaspoons honey, brown sugar or agave nectar
- 1 to 2 tablespoons pistachios, lightly toasted
- 3 ounces cherries 12 to 14, depending on the size, pitted and halved
- Milk or almond beverage as desired

Direction

- The night before you plan to make this dish, place the oatmeal in a large microwave-safe bowl or in a saucepan with the salt. Bring the water to a boil, and pour over the oatmeal. Cover tightly and leave overnight.
- In the morning, stir in the honey, pistachios and cherries. Cover and microwave three to five minutes, or simmer for 10 minutes or so until the oatmeal has absorbed the liquid remaining in the bowl. Stir in milk or almond beverage as desired.

---

118. Mushroom Quesadillas

Serving: Two quesadillas | Prep: | Cook: | Ready in: 20mins

Ingredients

- 1 tablespoon extra virgin olive oil
- 1 shallot, minced optional

- 6 ounces regular or wild mushrooms, trimmed and sliced about 1/4 inch thick
- 1 to 2 garlic cloves, minced
- 1 jalapeño or serrano chili, minced seeded for a milder flavor
- 1 tablespoon chopped cilantro or epazote
- Salt
- freshly ground pepper
- 4 corn tortillas
- 2 ounces grated Monterey Jack, Cheddar, or mixed cheeses 1/2 cup
- Salsa for serving optional

Direction

- Make the mushroom filling. Heat the oil over medium heat in a large, heavy frying pan. Add the shallot. Cook, stirring, until tender, about three minutes. Stir in the mushrooms. Cook, stirring, until tender and juicy, about five minutes. Add the garlic, chili, and salt and pepper. Cook, stirring, for another minute. Stir in the cilantro or epazote, and remove from the heat. Taste and adjust seasoning.
- In a microwave: Place a corn tortilla on a plate. Top with half the mushrooms, and spread in an even layer. Sprinkle on half the cheese, and top with another tortilla. Press down gently, then microwave for 1 to 1 1/2 minutes, until the cheese has melted. Remove from the microwave, cut into quarters or sixths and serve. Repeat with the remaining ingredients.
- In a pan: Place a corn tortilla in a pan. Top with half the mushrooms, and spread in an even layer. Sprinkle on half the cheese. Turn the heat to medium-high, and heat until the cheese begins to melt. Place another tortilla on top of the cheese, and press down lightly. Flip the quesadilla over in the pan, and heat for about 30 seconds or until the cheese has melted. Flip back over, and remove to a plate. Cut into quarters or sixths, and serve. Repeat with the remaining ingredients.

Nutrition Information

- 308: calories;

- 8 grams: monounsaturated fat;
- 2 grams: sugars;
- 29 grams: carbohydrates;
- 11 grams: protein;
- 408 milligrams: sodium;
- 17 grams: fat;
- 7 grams: dietary fiber;

119. Mushroom Stuffed Tomatoes

Serving: | Prep: | Cook: | Ready in: 41mins

Ingredients

- 2 tablespoons unsalted butter
- 2 tablespoons fruity olive oil
- ⅓ cup shallots, peeled and thinly sliced (4 to 6 shallots)
- 4 medium cloves garlic, peeled, minced and mashed
- 2 teaspoons kosher salt
- Freshly ground black pepper
- 6 large ripe tomatoes or 10 small ones (about 3 pounds)
- ¾ pound chanterelles, cleaned, trimmed and sliced 1/2-inch thick
- 1 teaspoon fresh marjoram leaves
- 2 teaspoons fresh thyme
- ⅓ cup orzo pasta
- ¼ cup fresh Italian parsley, minced
- 4 ounces mozzarella, cut into 1/4-inch cubes

Direction

- In a 10-inch quiche dish, combine butter, olive oil, shallots, garlic and salt. Cook, covered tightly with microwave plastic wrap, at 100 percent for 4 minutes.
- Core tomatoes. Cut a "lid" from the top of each, and, if necessary, a small slice from the bottom so that it will stand upright. Scoop flesh and seeds from each tomato to leave a shell for stuffing. Coarsely chop flesh and tops and set aside.

- Prick each tomato shell through the skin 5 to 6 times. Sprinkle the inside with salt and pepper. Arrange tomatoes in a ring in a dish just large enough to hold them and at least 2 inches deep.
- Stir chopped tomatoes, chanterelles, herbs and orzo into shallot mixture. Cover tightly with microwave plastic wrap and cook at 100 percent for 7 minutes. Uncover and stir in parsley, mozzarella and pepper. Divide mixture among tomato shells. Cover tightly with microwave plastic wrap and cook 100 percent for 5 minutes. Serve immediately, or let cool to room temperature and refrigerate; reheat, covered, for 1 minute 30 seconds before serving.

Nutrition Information

- 224: calories;
- 1 gram: polyunsaturated fat;
- 7 grams: sugars;
- 8 grams: protein;
- 6 grams: dietary fiber;
- 13 grams: fat;
- 0 grams: trans fat;
- 20 grams: carbohydrates;
- 765 milligrams: sodium;

---

120. Narial Jheenga (Bombay Coconut Shrimps)

Serving: Two servings | Prep: | Cook: | Ready in: 20mins

Ingredients

- ½ cup dried unsweetened coconut flakes
- ½ pound medium-large shrimps (about 14 to 16), shelled and deveined, tails intact
- ½ teaspoon minced garlic
- ½ teaspoon crushed or grated fresh ginger
- ½ teaspoon lemon juice
- ½ teaspoon coarsely ground black pepper
- ½ teaspoon ground cumin

- ¼ teaspoon coarse salt
- ¾ teaspoon cornstarch

Direction

- Spread out the coconut flakes in a 10-inch microwave-proof pie plate or dish. Toast, uncovered, at 100 percent power in a 650- to 700-watt microwave carousel oven for 3 to 5 minutes, or until lightly golden. Stir once during the cooking time. (The coconut will color unevenly.) Remove from the oven and set aside to cool.
- Place the shrimps in a bowl. Add the remaining ingredients and mix well to coat the shrimps. Lift the shrimps by their tails and dip them one at a time in the toasted coconut. Coat them evenly but lightly. Arrange the shrimps in the microwave-proof pie plate or dish, petal fashion, with the tails toward the center of the pan.
- Cook, covered, at 100 percent power in the microwave oven for 1 to 2 minutes, or until the shrimps are just done. They should be pink and firm. Remove and serve.

Nutrition Information

- 230: calories;
- 1 gram: polyunsaturated fat;
- 8 grams: carbohydrates;
- 4 grams: dietary fiber;
- 2 grams: sugars;
- 17 grams: protein;
- 651 milligrams: sodium;
- 12 grams: saturated fat;
- 0 grams: trans fat;
- 15 grams: fat;

---

121. New Classic Brownies

Serving: 16 brownies | Prep: | Cook: | Ready in: 40mins

Ingredients

- 8 tablespoons unsalted butter
- 4 ounces unsweetened chocolate
- 1 ¼ cups sugar
- 1 teaspoon vanilla extract
- ¼ teaspoon salt
- 2 eggs
- ½ cup all-purpose flour
- ⅔ cup lightly toasted walnuts or pecans (optional)

Direction

- Preheat oven to 400 degrees. Line an 8-inch-square metal baking pan with foil. In top of a double boiler set over barely simmering water, or on low power in a microwave, melt butter and chocolate together. Stir often, and remove from heat when a few lumps remain. Stir until smooth.
- Stir in sugar, vanilla and salt. Stir in eggs one at a time, followed by flour. Stir until very smooth, about 1 minute, until mixture pulls away from sides of bowl. Add nuts, if using. Scrape batter into prepared pan and bake 20 minutes.
- Meanwhile, prepare a water bath: Pour ice water into a large roasting pan or kitchen sink to a depth of about 1 inch. Remove pan from oven and place in water bath, being careful not to splash water on brownies. Let cool completely, then lift out and cut into 1-inch squares or wrap in foil.

Nutrition Information

- 180: calories;
- 0 grams: polyunsaturated fat;
- 3 grams: monounsaturated fat;
- 2 grams: protein;
- 10 grams: fat;
- 6 grams: saturated fat;
- 21 grams: carbohydrates;
- 1 gram: dietary fiber;
- 16 grams: sugars;
- 47 milligrams: sodium;

122. New Potatoes

Serving: 8 servings | Prep: | Cook: | Ready in: 18mins

Ingredients

- 2 pounds small new potatoes
- ½ cup water

Direction

- Scrub potatoes and place in water in a 1 1/2-quart souffle dish. Cover tightly with microwavable plastic wrap. Cook at 100 percent power in a high-power oven for 14 minutes. Prick plastic to release steam.
- Remove from oven and uncover. Let cool to room temperature.

Nutrition Information

- 87: calories;
- 1 gram: sugars;
- 7 milligrams: sodium;
- 0 grams: polyunsaturated fat;
- 20 grams: carbohydrates;
- 2 grams: protein;

123. Oatmeal And Teff With Cinnamon And Dried Fruit

Serving: Serves 1 | Prep: | Cook: | Ready in: 5mins

Ingredients

- For 1 generous bowl
- ⅓ cup rolled oats
- 1 tablespoon teff
- Salt to taste (I use a generous pinch)
- ⅛ teaspoon ground cinnamon
- 1 tablespoon chopped dried apricots and/or golden raisins (more to taste)
- ⅔ cup water

- 1 teaspoon honey, plus additional to taste for drizzling
- ½ tablespoon chopped toasted skinned hazelnuts or almonds
- Optional toppings: milk, grated apple or pear

Direction

- The night before, stir together rolled oats, teff, salt, cinnamon and chopped apricots or raisins in a medium microwave-safe bowl. Bring water to a boil and pour over mixture. Add honey and stir, then cover bowl with a plate.
- In the morning, microwave mixture for 2 minutes on 100 percent power. Remove bowl from microwave and carefully remove plate (bowl will be hot and steam will rise from cereal). Stir mixture, cover again and return to microwave. Heat for 1 to 2 minutes longer, until mixture is no longer watery.
- Transfer to a serving dish and sprinkle chopped nuts over the top. Add other toppings of your choice and serve.

124.   Orange Poached Figs

Serving: 4 servings | Prep: | Cook: | Ready in: 10mins

Ingredients

- 7 tablespoons fresh orange juice
- 3 tablespoons fresh lemon juice
- 3 tablespoons sugar
- ⅛ teaspoon freshly ground black pepper
- 1 2-inch piece vanilla bean, split lengthwise
- 12 ripe figs, preferably black

Direction

- In a small bowl, stir together orange juice, lemon juice, sugar, pepper and vanilla bean.
- Place an inverted 3-cup souffle dish in the center of a 10-inch pie plate to create a ring mold. Pour the liquid mixture into the dish.
- Arrange the figs in a circle, leaning them against the souffle dish with the stems facing

up. Invert a second 10-inch pie plate over the first to form a cover.
- Cook at 100 percent power in a high-power oven for 5 minutes.
- Remove from oven and uncover. Let figs cool before serving warm, or let cool completely. Serve with vanilla ice cream or heavy cream.

Nutrition Information

- 169: calories;
- 43 grams: carbohydrates;
- 5 grams: dietary fiber;
- 37 grams: sugars;
- 2 milligrams: sodium;
- 1 gram: protein;
- 0 grams: polyunsaturated fat;

125.   Parsley Sauce

Serving: One and a half cups | Prep: | Cook: | Ready in: 15mins

Ingredients

- 1 ½ cups parsley leaves (preferably flat-leaf)
- ½ cup, plus 1 1/2 tablespoons, canned or fresh chicken broth
- 1 tablespoon cornstarch
- ½ teaspoon kosher salt
- ½ cup heavy cream

Direction

- Place the parsley and a half-cup of broth in a food processor. Process for one minute. Scrape mixture into a two-cup glass measure.
- Combine the remaining broth with the cornstarch and stir into the parsley mixture. Cover tightly with microwave plastic wrap. Cook at 100 percent for four minutes.
- Uncover. Stir in salt. Allow to cool slightly. Whip the cream to soft peaks and fold into the parsley mixture. Serve with the demitasse carrot custards.

Nutrition Information

- 159: calories;
- 2 grams: protein;
- 174 milligrams: sodium;
- 15 grams: fat;
- 9 grams: saturated fat;
- 4 grams: monounsaturated fat;
- 1 gram: sugars;
- 6 grams: carbohydrates;

126.   Pastichio

Serving: 6 to 8 servings | Prep: | Cook: |Ready in: 50mins

Ingredients

- ¾ pound lean ground lamb
- 4 cloves garlic, smashed, peeled and minced
- ¼ pound ripe tomatoes, cored and coarsely chopped
- 1 tablespoon tomato paste
- ½ teaspoon ground cumin
- ½ teaspoon oregano
- ½ teaspoon thyme
- Pinch cinnamon
- 2 teaspoons coarse kosher salt
- Freshly ground pepper to taste
- ¾ cup dry bread crumbs
- 3 cups cooked elbow macaroni (16 ounces dried)
- 5 eggs
- 1 cup milk
- 1 cup heavy cream
- Pinch nutmeg
- 2 ounces grated Gruyere
- 4 ounces crumbled feta

Direction

- Preheat broiler. Place rack 6 inches from heat source.

- In a 12-inch oval glass or ceramic casserole 2 1/2 inches deep, combine lamb, garlic, tomatoes, tomato paste, cumin, oregano, thyme, cinnamon, 1 teaspoon salt and pepper. Cook, uncovered at 100 percent power for 5 minutes, stirring twice to break up meat. Remove from oven and stir in 1/2 cup bread crumbs.
- Spread macaroni on top of meat. Whisk together remaining ingredients, including 1 teaspoon salt, pepper and 1/4 cup bread crumbs. Pour over macaroni. Poke handle of a wooden spoon through mixture to let liquid reach all parts of dish. Cover tightly with microwave plastic wrap. Cook at 100 percent power for 5 minutes. Pierce plastic so steam can escape.
- Uncover. Stir macaroni layer. Cover tightly with plastic wrap. Cook at 100 percent power for 5 minutes. Pierce plastic, uncover and cook 2 minutes longer.
- If desired, broil until top is browned. Allow to stand at room temperature 10 minutes before serving.

Nutrition Information

- 478: calories;
- 29 grams: carbohydrates;
- 540 milligrams: sodium;
- 10 grams: monounsaturated fat;
- 0 grams: trans fat;
- 2 grams: dietary fiber;
- 5 grams: sugars;
- 21 grams: protein;
- 31 grams: fat;
- 16 grams: saturated fat;

127.   Peach Sorbet

Serving: 9 servings | Prep: | Cook: |Ready in: 25mins

Ingredients

- 6 medium peaches (2 pounds)
- 3 tablespoons fresh lemon juice
- 2 cups sugar
- 2 cups water

Direction

- Fill a medium saucepan with water and bring to a boil. Place peaches in water for about 15 seconds. Remove with slotted spoon.
- Place lemon juice in a bowl. Slip skin off peaches with a paring knife. Cut peaches in half and remove pits. Reserve skin and pits. As you work, add peaches to the bowl and coat with lemon juice.
- Stir together sugar, water, peach skin and pits in a 2 1/2-quart souffle dish. Cook, uncovered, at 100 percent in a high-power oven for 3 minutes. Stir thoroughly, making sure there are no grains on the bottom of the dish. Cover with a lid or microwave plastic wrap. Cook for 6 minutes. Prick plastic, if used, to release steam.
- Remove from oven and uncover. Let cool. Strain and refrigerate until cold, several hours or overnight.
- While syrup is cooking, place peach flesh and lemon juice in a blender. Blend until very smooth, stopping several times to scrape down sides of jar. Refrigerate until cold.
- Whisk peach puree and syrup together. Place in an ice-cream machine and freeze according to manufacturer's instructions.

Nutrition Information

- 211: calories;
- 3 milligrams: sodium;
- 0 grams: polyunsaturated fat;
- 54 grams: carbohydrates;
- 1 gram: protein;
- 53 grams: sugars;

128. Peasant Tomato Soup

Serving: 4 cups | Prep: | Cook: | Ready in: 17mins

Ingredients

- ¼ pound carrots (2 medium size), trimmed, scraped and cut in 2-inch pieces
- ¼ pound yellow onion (1 small or 1/2 large), peeled and quartered
- ¼ pound fennel bulb, trimmed and pared with a potato peeler
- 3 medium-size cloves garlic, peeled and smashed
- 2 tablespoons of olive oil
- 1 pound canned tomatoes with thick puree
- 1 tablespoon cornstarch
- 2 cups chicken broth
- 1 teaspoon coarse kosher salt
- 1 ½ tablespoons freshly squeezed lemon juice
- Fresh basil, washed and shredded, to taste

Direction

- Coarsely chop carrots, onion, fennel and garlic in food processor. In a 2 1/2-quart ceramic or glass souffle dish, stir chopped vegetables and oil until well mixed. Cook, uncovered, at 100 percent for 4 minutes.
- Meanwhile puree contents of tomato can in food processor. Dissolve cornstarch in chicken broth. Add pureed tomatoes and chicken broth mixture to vegetables. Cover tightly with polyvinyl plastic wrap. Cook at 100 percent for 7 minutes. Season with remaining ingredients.

Nutrition Information

- 165: calories;
- 1 gram: polyunsaturated fat;
- 6 grams: monounsaturated fat;
- 19 grams: carbohydrates;
- 4 grams: dietary fiber;
- 5 grams: protein;
- 778 milligrams: sodium;
- 9 grams: sugars;

129. Peppermint Bark

Serving: About 1 1/2 pounds | Prep: | Cook: | Ready in: 5hours

Ingredients

- 1 pound/455 grams good-quality semisweet chocolate (not chips), chopped
- 8 ounces/225 grams good-quality white chocolate (not chips), chopped
- ½ to ¾ teaspoon oil-based peppermint extract, such as Simply Organic brand
- ½ cup/75 grams crushed candy canes

Direction

- Line a rimmed baking sheet with parchment paper and set aside. Set 12 ounces/340 grams semisweet chocolate in a microwave-safe bowl and microwave it in 5- to 25-second bursts, stirring occasionally, until it is melted and the temperature registers between 114 degrees and 118 degrees on an instant-read thermometer. Chocolate burns easily in the microwave, so go slowly. Try fewer seconds as the temperature starts getting close so that you don't overshoot the mark. (If you're a few degrees over, just keeping stirring the chocolate until it cools to the proper temperature.)
- Remove the bowl from the microwave and gradually stir in the remaining 4 ounces/115 grams semisweet chocolate until the temperature has come down to 88 to 89 degrees. (After a bit of practice you can actually see and feel the chocolate fall into temper. It takes on a slightly looser quality and becomes shinier. Be patient, this can take up to 10 to 12 minutes with some chocolate.) Now quickly pour the chocolate out onto the prepared pan and spread it into an even layer. Let the chocolate stand at room temperature until the layer has set, about 1 hour. (You can also refrigerate until set, about 30 minutes.)
- Now set 6 ounces/170 grams white chocolate in a microwave-safe bowl and microwave it in 5- to 25-second bursts, stirring occasionally, until it is melted and the temperature registers between 105 degrees and 110 degrees on an instant-read thermometer.
- Remove the bowl from the microwave and gradually stir in the remaining 2 ounces/55 grams white chocolate until the temperature has come down to about 85 degrees. Quickly stir in the peppermint extract. Drizzle the white chocolate mixture evenly over the semisweet chocolate. Immediately sprinkle with the candy cane.
- Let stand at room temperature until completely set, about 4 hours. To serve, break into pieces. Refrigerate leftover pieces as necessary.

Nutrition Information

- 313: calories;
- 39 grams: carbohydrates;
- 22 milligrams: sodium;
- 11 grams: saturated fat;
- 1 gram: polyunsaturated fat;
- 3 grams: protein;
- 35 grams: sugars;
- 19 grams: fat;
- 6 grams: monounsaturated fat;

130. Pesto Sauce

Serving: 2/3 cup sauce (enough for pasta for 4) | Prep: | Cook: | Ready in: 15mins

Ingredients

- 1 whole bulb garlic, the cloves separated, peeled and smashed
- ½ cup chicken broth, prepared by any standard recipe, or canned

- 2 cups fresh basil leaves
- 1 tablespoon olive oil
- ½ teaspoon kosher salt (optional; skip if using canned broth)

Direction

- Place garlic and broth in a 4-cup glass measure. Cover tightly with microwave plastic wrap. Cook at 100 percent power for 8 minutes (15 minutes in a small oven).
- Remove from the oven. Pierce plastic with tip of a small knife to release steam, then carefully remove plastic. Scrape mixture into a blender. Blend until smooth. With motor running, add the basil, then the oil and, if desired, salt. Blend well.

Nutrition Information

- 186: calories;
- 404 milligrams: sodium;
- 12 grams: fat;
- 2 grams: sugars;
- 8 grams: monounsaturated fat;
- 1 gram: dietary fiber;
- 17 grams: carbohydrates;
- 6 grams: protein;

131. Poached Lamb With Garlic

Serving: 10 to 12 servings | Prep: | Cook: | Ready in: 40mins

Ingredients

- 5 pounds lamb, shoulder or leg; trimmed, boned and rolled
- 2 whole bulbs garlic, the cloves separated, peeled and smashed
- 1 cup chicken broth, prepared by any standard recipe, or canned chicken broth
- 1 cup heavy cream

- 1 tablespoon cornstarch dissolved in 2 tablespoons cold water
- 1 ½ teaspoons kosher salt (add less if using canned broth)
- Freshly ground black pepper

Direction

- Place the lamb, fat side up, in a 2-quart round or oval souffle dish with sides at least 2 1/2 inches deep. Sprinkle garlic cloves around and under the lamb. Pour the broth and cream over all. Cover tightly with microwave plastic wrap. Cook at 100 percent power for 15 minutes.
- Pierce the plastic with the tip of a small knife to release steam, then uncover carefully. Turn the lamb over, re-cover, and cook 15 minutes longer.
- Remove the lamb from the oven, pierce the plastic, and uncover. Place the lamb on a platter, and cover with plastic wrap. Let stand for 15 minutes while you prepare the sauce.
- Scrape the cooking liquid and garlic into the bowl of a food processor, and puree until smooth. Pour back into cooking dish. Stir in the cornstarch mixture. Cook, uncovered, in the microwave oven for 5 minutes. Season to taste with salt and pepper.
- Slice the lamb 1/4 to 1/2 inch thick. Pour the sauce onto a platter, and arange the lamb on top. Serve warm or at room temperature.

132. Poached Plums

Serving: 6 servings | Prep: | Cook: | Ready in: 22mins

Ingredients

- 2 cups sugar
- 2 cups water
- 1-inch piece cinnamon stick
- 4 3-by-1-inch strips lemon zest
- 1 small vanilla bean
- 6 small, firm red plums (about 1 pound)

Direction

- Stir sugar and water together in a 2 1/2-quart souffle dish. Add cinnamon stick. Cook, uncovered, at 100 percent in a high-power oven for 3 minutes. Stir thoroughly, making sure there are no grains on the bottom of the dish. Cover with a lid or microwave plastic wrap. Cook for 6 minutes. Prick plastic, if used, to release steam.
- Remove from oven and uncover. Stir in lemon zest and vanilla bean. Add plums. Cook, covered, at 100 percent power in a high-power oven for 8 minutes.
- Remove from oven and uncover. Let cool. Remove vanilla bean and store, tightly covered, in the refrigerator.
- Serve chilled, in a bowl, with some of the syrup.

Nutrition Information

- 294: calories;
- 0 grams: polyunsaturated fat;
- 75 grams: carbohydrates;
- 1 gram: protein;
- 74 grams: sugars;
- 4 milligrams: sodium;

---

133.   Polenta

Serving: Serves 4 | Prep: | Cook: | Ready in: 1hours30mins

Ingredients

- For the easy oven-baked polenta
- 1 cup polenta
- 1 quart water
- 1 teaspoon salt
- 1 tablespoon unsalted butter
- For the microwave polenta
- ¾ cup polenta
- ¾ teaspoon salt
- 3 cups water
- 1 tablespoon unsalted butter

Direction

- Preheat the oven to 350 degrees. Combine the polenta, water and salt in a 2-quart baking dish. Stir together, and place in the oven. Bake 50 minutes. Remove from the oven, and stir in the butter. Use a fork or a spatula to stir the polenta well, and return to the oven for 10 minutes. Remove from the oven, and stir again. Carefully taste a little bit of the polenta; if the grains are not completely soft, return to the oven for 10 minutes. Serve right away for soft polenta, or let sit five minutes for a stiffer polenta. Spoon onto a plate. Make a depression in the middle, and serve with the topping of your choice or plain, as a side dish. Alternatively, for grilling or use in another recipe, allow to chill and stiffen in the baking dish, or scrape into a lightly oiled or buttered bread pan and chill.
- Combine the polenta, salt and water in a 2 1/2- to 3-quart microwave-safe bowl, and stir together. Cover the bowl with a plate, and place in the microwave. Microwave on high for eight minutes. Remove from the microwave carefully, wearing oven mitts, as the bowl will be quite hot. Carefully remove the plate from the top, and allow the steam to escape. Stir in the butter, and mix well with a fork. Cover the bowl again with the plate and return to the microwave. Microwave on high for three minutes. Again, remove from the microwave carefully, wearing oven mitts. Carefully remove the plate from the top, and allow the steam to escape. Stir the polenta, and return to the microwave for three more minutes. Carefully remove from the microwave. Stir and serve, or pour into a lightly buttered bread pan and allow to cool, then slice and grill or sear in a lightly oiled pan.

Nutrition Information

- 305: calories;
- 7 grams: fat;
- 2 grams: monounsaturated fat;
- 1 gram: sugars;
- 5 grams: protein;
- 1040 milligrams: sodium;
- 4 grams: saturated fat;
- 0 grams: trans fat;
- 55 grams: carbohydrates;
- 3 grams: dietary fiber;

134.   Polenta Lasagna

Serving: 5 servings | Prep: | Cook: | Ready in: 24mins

Ingredients

- The filling:
- 2 ounces onion, peeled and cut into 1-inch pieces
- 1 clove garlic, smashed and peeled
- 2 teaspoons olive oil
- 2 ounces eggplant, cut into 1-inch pieces
- 4 ounces zucchini, cut into 1-inch pieces
- ½ cup tomato puree
- Pinch dried oregano
- Pinch dried thyme
- 1 teaspoon kosher salt
- Pinch freshly ground black pepper
- 1 tablespoon chopped fresh basil
- The lasagna:
- Basic polenta (see recipe), chilled and cut into rectangles
- 5 ounces mozzarella (whole-milk or part-skim), cut into 5 slices

Direction

- Place onion and garlic in the bowl of a food processor. Process until finely chopped. Scrape into a 10-inch quiche dish, and add the oil. Stir to coat the onion and garlic. In a 650- to 700-watt oven cook, uncovered, at 100 percent power for 2 minutes.
- While onion and garlic are cooking, finely chop the eggplant and zucchini in the food processor. Stir into the onion mixture. Cook, uncovered, at 100 percent power for 4 minutes.
- Leaving the dish in oven, add the tomato puree, oregano, thyme and salt. Cook, uncovered, at 100 percent power for 3 minutes. Remove from the oven, stir in the pepper and basil, and set aside.
- Place half the polenta slices spoke-fashion in a 14-by-11-by-2-inch dish. Top each slice with a fifth of the vegetable mixture. Then top each with a piece of mozzarella and another slice of polenta. Cook uncovered at 100 percent power for 5 minutes.

Nutrition Information

- 121: calories;
- 4 grams: saturated fat;
- 0 grams: polyunsaturated fat;
- 235 milligrams: sodium;
- 8 grams: fat;
- 3 grams: sugars;
- 5 grams: carbohydrates;
- 1 gram: dietary fiber;
- 7 grams: protein;

135.   Popcorn

Serving: | Prep: | Cook: | Ready in: 10mins

Ingredients

- Fry minced slab bacon
- popcorn
- rosemary or thyme
- black pepper

Direction

- Fry minced slab bacon until crisp. Make popcorn. Toss together (fat included) with chopped rosemary or thyme and lots of black pepper. Best served hot.

136. Popcorn Crunch

Serving: 1 1/2 pounds | Prep: | Cook: | Ready in: 55mins

Ingredients

- Vegetable oil for coating pan
- 2 cups granulated sugar
- 1 cup light corn syrup
- 1 cup water
- 1 ½ cups pecans
- 4 cups cooked, unsalted popcorn

Direction

- Preheat conventional oven to 350 degrees. Oil a large baking sheet and a large spoon. Set aside.
- Stir sugar, corn syrup and water together in a 2 1/2-quart souffle dish. Cook, uncovered, at 100 percent power in a high-power microwave oven for 4 minutes. Stir.
- Cover tightly with microwave plastic wrap. Cook for 31 minutes.
- While syrup is cooking, place pecans on a baking sheet and bake for 10 minutes, stirring once. Set aside.
- Remove syrup dish from oven. Prick plastic to release steam. Uncover and let stand for 2 minutes. Use the spoon to carefully stir in popcorn and nuts. Let stand for 5 minutes, turning the popcorn over in the mixture from time to time to make sure that the popcorn and the nuts are well coated.
- Spoon the mixture out onto the baking sheet. Use the back of the spoon to spread the popcorn mixture into an even layer. Let harden and cool, about 15 minutes.
- When cool, break into chunks with a wooden mallet or rolling pin. Store in an airtight container.

Nutrition Information

- 320: calories;
- 1 gram: protein;
- 3 grams: polyunsaturated fat;
- 56 grams: sugars;
- 11 grams: fat;
- 58 grams: carbohydrates;
- 19 milligrams: sodium;
- 0 grams: trans fat;
- 6 grams: monounsaturated fat;

137. Pork Loin In Rhubarb Sauce

Serving: 8 servings | Prep: | Cook: | Ready in: 1hours

Ingredients

- 1 ½ tablespoons unsalted butter
- 1 pound onions (3 medium-size), peeled, halved and sliced thin (3 cups)
- 1 boneless pork loin roast (about 3 1/2 pounds, 10 inches long and 4 inches in diameter)
- 2 teaspoons kosher salt
- Freshly ground black pepper to taste
- 1 ¼ pounds rhubarb, trimmed and cut on the diagonal in 1/8-inch thick slices (3 cups)

Direction

- Place butter in a 5-quart casserole with a tight-fitting lid. Cook, uncovered, at 100 percent power in a high-power microwave oven for 2 minutes. Stir in onions. Cook, uncovered, for 4 minutes.
- Sprinkle roast with the salt and some pepper. Remove casserole from oven. Stir in rhubarb. Place the pork, fat side down, diagonally in the casserole, pushing the onion mixture around the roast. Cook, covered, for 10 minutes.

- Uncover and turn roast over. Re-cover and cook for 10 minutes. Uncover and turn roast again. Cook, uncovered, for 15 minutes.
- While roast is cooking, preheat broiler. Remove casserole from oven. Transfer pork to a small roasting pan, fat side up. Place under broiler until top browns, about 2 minutes.
- Let roast stand for 10 minutes. Remove strings. Cut in 1/4-inch thick slices. Stir several grinds of pepper into the sauce. Pour a generous 1/4-cup sauce onto each plate. Place two slices of pork over sauce and serve.

Nutrition Information

- 511: calories;
- 0 grams: trans fat;
- 8 grams: carbohydrates;
- 3 grams: sugars;
- 60 grams: protein;
- 604 milligrams: sodium;
- 25 grams: fat;
- 6 grams: monounsaturated fat;
- 2 grams: dietary fiber;

138.   Pork And Pistachio Pate

Serving: 8 one-inch slices | Prep: | Cook: | Ready in: 16mins

Ingredients

- 1 ½ pounds pork sausage meat
- ½ cup cold butter, cut into pieces
- 4 ounces yellow onions, peeled and cut into quarters
- 3 cloves garlic, smashed, peeled and chopped
- 2 tablespoons brandy
- 2 ½ teaspoons dried thyme
- 1 ½ teaspoons dried oregano
- 1 teaspoon ground fennel seeds
- ¾ teaspoon ground black pepper
- Salt to taste (optional)

- 2 ounces toasted pistachio nuts (see Micro-Tips)

Direction

- Place all ingredients except salt and pistachio nuts in bowl of food processor and process until smooth. Wrap 1 teaspoon of mixture in microwave plastic wrap. Cook at 100 percent power in a 650- to 700- watt oven for 45 seconds. Remove from oven and uncover. Taste for saltiness and add salt to mixture if desired.
- Scrape pate mixture into a bowl and stir in pistachio nuts. Transfer to a glass or ceramic loaf pan, 9 by 5 by 3 inches, that either has a nonstick surface or has been sprayed with nonstick vegetable spray. Smooth out surface with a spatula. Cover pan with microwave plastic wrap. Cook at 100 percent power for 12 minutes. Prick plastic to release steam.
- Remove from oven and uncover. Cut a piece of cardboard to just fit the loaf pan and cover with aluminum foil. Place over pate in pan. Refrigerate with 2 or 3 heavy cans on top overnight.
- Run a thin knife around the inside edge of pan to loosen pate. Invert onto a serving plate.

Nutrition Information

- 403: calories;
- 632 milligrams: sodium;
- 36 grams: fat;
- 14 grams: saturated fat;
- 13 grams: monounsaturated fat;
- 2 grams: sugars;
- 15 grams: protein;
- 1 gram: dietary fiber;
- 5 grams: carbohydrates;

139. Portuguese Fish Stew

Serving: Six main-course portions or 12 first-course portions | Prep: | Cook: | Ready in: 1hours16mins

Ingredients

- ¼ cup olive oil
- 2 pounds potatoes, peeled and sliced 1/4-inch thick, about 5 cups
- 2 ½ pounds mackerel, filleted, with heads and bones cut into 2-inch pieces
- 3 ½ cups dry white wine
- 20 cloves garlic, smashed and peeled
- 1 ¼ pounds kale, stemmed, washed and cut into 1-inch slices
- 1 ½ tablespoons kosher salt
- Freshly ground black pepper, to taste

Direction

- Stir together oil and potatoes in a 5-quart glass or ceramic casserole. Cover securely with microwave plastic wrap or a tightly fitting lid. Cook at 100 percent power for 4 minutes in a 650- to 700-watt oven. If using plastic, prick to release steam.
- Remove from oven. Place fish bones and heads on a double thickness of cheesecloth and tie securely with string. Add to casserole along with 2 1/2 cups of the wine and garlic. Cover and cook for 22 minutes, stirring twice.
- While potato mixture is cooking, halve fillets lengthwise and remove pin bones; try a tweezers. Cut across into 2-inch chunks.
- If using plastic, prick to release steam. Remove casserole from oven and uncover. Discard fish heads and bones in cheesecloth. Place fish over potatoes and top with kale. Re-cover and cook for 17 minutes. If using plastic, prick to release steam.
- Remove from oven and uncover. Stir in remaining 1-cup wine, salt and pepper to taste, breaking up the fish as you stir. Re-cover and cook for 3 minutes more or until hot.

Nutrition Information

- 757: calories;
- 8 grams: polyunsaturated fat;
- 17 grams: monounsaturated fat;
- 43 grams: protein;
- 7 grams: dietary fiber;
- 5 grams: sugars;
- 1366 milligrams: sodium;
- 36 grams: fat;

140. Pumpkin Squash

Serving: 10 - 12 servings | Prep: | Cook: | Ready in: 1hours

Ingredients

- 7 pounds pumpkin, cut in 4-by-5-inch pieces, or 5 acorn squash (1 1/4 pounds each), cut in half lengthwise, seeds and fibers removed
- ½ cup water
- 5 large eggs
- ¼ cup heavy cream
- 1 cup cake flour
- 2 teaspoons baking soda
- 1 ½ teaspoons dried sage
- 2 teaspoons salt
- Freshly ground black pepper to taste

Direction

- Cook pumpkin or squash in the water for 30 minutes. Scrape out flesh. It will instantly turn into a puree. Thoroughly drain through a fine-mesh sieve. Reserve liquid for another use. Transfer to an oval dish.
- Whisk eggs into squash. Add remaining ingredients and whisk until combined well, scraping edges and bottom of dish.
- Cover tightly with microwave-oven plastic wrap. Cook at 100 percent power in a 650- to 700-watt oven for 5 minutes. Prick plastic to release steam.
- Uncover and stir well. Smooth mixture into an even layer. Cover and cook for 4 to 5 minutes. Prick plastic to release steam.

- Remove from oven. Uncover. Cut into slices and serve warm.

Nutrition Information

- 160: calories;
- 632 milligrams: sodium;
- 0 grams: trans fat;
- 1 gram: polyunsaturated fat;
- 27 grams: carbohydrates;
- 8 grams: sugars;
- 6 grams: protein;
- 4 grams: fat;
- 2 grams: dietary fiber;

141.   Quesadilla With Mushroom Ragoût And Chipotles

Serving: 2 quesadillas | Prep: | Cook: | Ready in: 10mins

Ingredients

- 6 tablespoons mushroom ragoût
- 1 teaspoon chopped canned chipotle in adobo (more to taste)
- 4 corn tortillas
- 1 ½ ounces grated Monterey Jack or Gruyère (about 1/3 cup)

Direction

- Stir the chopped chipotles into the mushroom ragoût. Taste and add more if you want more spice.
- Using a microwave: Place a corn tortilla on a plate. Top with a heaped tablespoon of the grated cheese. Add half the mushrooms and spread in an even layer. Sprinkle another heaped tablespoon of the cheese over the mushrooms and top with another tortilla. Press down gently. Repeat with the remaining ingredients. Microwave for 1 to 1 1/2 minutes, until the cheese has melted. Remove from the

microwave, cut into quarters, and serve. Using a pan: Place a corn tortilla in a pan. Top with a heaped tablespoon of the cheese and half the mushrooms and spread in an even layer. Sprinkle on another heaped tablespoon the cheese. Turn the heat on medium-high and heat until the cheese begins to melt. Place the remaining tortilla on top of the cheese and press down lightly. Flip the quesadilla over in the pan and heat for about 30 seconds, or until the cheese has melted. Flip back over and remove to a plate. Cut into quarters or sixths, and serve. Repeat with the remaining ingredients.

Nutrition Information

- 190: calories;
- 22 grams: carbohydrates;
- 9 grams: protein;
- 182 milligrams: sodium;
- 8 grams: fat;
- 4 grams: saturated fat;
- 2 grams: monounsaturated fat;
- 1 gram: sugars;
- 3 grams: dietary fiber;

142.   Raspberry Pudding

Serving: Two and a half cups | Prep: | Cook: | Ready in: 2hours15mins

Ingredients

- ½ cup milk
- 3 tablespoons cornstarch
- 1 cup heavy cream
- ¼ cup granulated sugar
- 1 10-ounce package frozen raspberries in light syrup, defrosted and drained in a sieve set over a bowl
- 1 tablespoon fresh lemon juice

Direction

- Combine the milk and cornstarch in a small bowl, making sure there are no lumps. Stir in the cream and sugar and pour the mixture into a 2 1/2-quart souffle dish. Cover tightly with microwave plastic wrap. Cook at 100 percent power in a 650- to 700-watt microwave oven for 4 minutes. Prick the plastic to release steam.
- Remove from oven. Scrape into a food processor and add raspberries, discarding syrup. Puree until very smooth. Divide among ramekins or transfer to a serving bowl and refrigerate for 2 hours or until chilled.

Nutrition Information

- 222: calories;
- 16 grams: fat;
- 4 grams: monounsaturated fat;
- 3 grams: dietary fiber;
- 2 grams: protein;
- 1 gram: polyunsaturated fat;
- 20 grams: carbohydrates;
- 13 grams: sugars;
- 25 milligrams: sodium;
- 10 grams: saturated fat;

143. Raspberry Rice Pudding

Serving: 6 to 8 servings | Prep: | Cook: | Ready in: 47mins

Ingredients

- 1 ½ cups long grain rice (not instant or converted)
- 5 eggs
- 1 cup heavy cream
- 1 cup milk
- Pinch nutmeg
- ⅓ cup sugar
- ½ pint fresh raspberries
- 1 teaspoon vanilla

- 2 tablespoons raspberry eau-de-vie (white raspberry brandy)

Direction

- Cook rice in boiling water on top of the stove for 15 minutes. Rinse with cold water and drain.
- Whisk together eggs, cream, milk, nutmeg and sugar. In a 9 1/2-inch oval dish 2 1/2 inches deep, combine egg mixture and rice. Cover with plastic wrap. Cook at 100 percent power for 5 minutes. Stir together raspberries, vanilla and eau-de-vie.
- Pierce plastic to release steam. Uncover and stir custard until smooth. Lightly stir in raspberries and flavorings. Cover with microwave plastic wrap. Cook at 100 percent power for 5 minutes. Pierce plastic, uncover and cook 2 minutes longer. If desired, brown under broiler.

Nutrition Information

- 337: calories;
- 15 grams: fat;
- 8 grams: protein;
- 0 grams: trans fat;
- 12 grams: sugars;
- 4 grams: monounsaturated fat;
- 1 gram: polyunsaturated fat;
- 41 grams: carbohydrates;
- 2 grams: dietary fiber;
- 65 milligrams: sodium;

144. Raspberry Rose Truffles

Serving: About 95 truffles | Prep: | Cook: | Ready in: 3hours

Ingredients

- 1 ½ cups fresh raspberries
- 1 tablespoon sugar
- ¼ cup rose syrup (see note)

- 1 pound plus 12 ounces bittersweet chocolate, finely chopped
- 1 ¾ cups heavy cream
- 7 tablespoons unsalted butter at room temperature, cut into pieces
- Cocoa for dusting (optional)

Direction

- In a food processor or blender, purée raspberries with sugar. Push mixture through a fine mesh sieve; discard solids. Stir rose syrup into raspberry purée and set aside.
- Place 12 ounces chocolate in a heatproof bowl. In a saucepan, bring cream to a simmer. Pour cream over chocolate and let rest 3 minutes. Starting in center, whisk together chocolate and cream. Continue to whisk until mixture turns dark and shiny and has consistency of mayonnaise. Cool until slightly warm.
- Whisk butter into chocolate mixture until melted, then stir in raspberry mixture. Refrigerate until mixture is as thick as icing, 30 minutes to an hour.
- Transfer mixture to a pastry bag with a large plain tip or to a resealable plastic bag with a corner cut off. Line a baking sheet with parchment or waxed paper and squeeze 1 1/4-inch chocolate drops (a bit larger than a Hershey's Kiss) onto paper. Refrigerate drops until firm, about 1 hour.
- Using your hands, roll chocolate drops into balls, then return them to baking sheet and refrigerate for another 15 minutes, until their surfaces are matte.
- Meanwhile, to make the coating, set aside 1/4 of the remaining chocolate. Place the rest of the chopped chocolate in a microwave-proof bowl. Microwave on high for 3 minutes, stopping every 15 seconds to stir. Chocolate should feel very warm to the touch (115 to 120 degrees). Add reserved chopped chocolate to bowl; stir until mixture is melted and smooth and chocolate has cooled to 82 degrees. Return chocolate to microwave on high for another 5 seconds. Stir again.
- Line another baking sheet with waxed or parchment paper. Use a fork to lower chocolate balls one by one into chocolate coating. Turn each one to coat, drain off excess, and place balls on parchment paper. If the melted chocolate cools too much and thickens, return it to microwave for 3 to 5 seconds, and stir well.
- Let truffles rest for at least 20 minutes. If desired, roll truffles in cocoa powder before serving. Store in airtight containers in refrigerator for up to 2 weeks. Bring to room temperature before removing lid.

Nutrition Information

- 66: calories;
- 6 grams: carbohydrates;
- 1 gram: dietary fiber;
- 3 milligrams: sodium;
- 5 grams: sugars;
- 3 grams: saturated fat;
- 0 grams: protein;
- 2 grams: monounsaturated fat;

145.   Red Snapper With Hot Pepper And Cilantro

Serving: 2 main-course servings | Prep: | Cook: | Ready in: 16mins

Ingredients

- 1 jalapeno pepper, stemmed, seeded and sliced across into thin rings
- 4 nickel-size slices of peeled fresh ginger
- ¼ cup cilantro leaves, stems reserved with the root end trimmed
- 3 tablespoons fresh lime juice
- 1 2-pound red snapper
- Large pinch kosher salt

Direction

- Place half of the jalapeno rings, half of the ginger and the cilantro stems in the cavity of the fish. Place the fish in a 14-by-9-by-2-inch oval dish. Coat both sides of fish with the lime juice. It is fine for the tail to hang over the edge of the dish. Scatter the remaining jalapeno, ginger and cilantro leaves around the fish.
- Cover the dish tightly with microwave plastic wrap, making sure the tail is well covered and plastic adheres to dish. Cook at 100 percent power in a high-power oven for 11 minutes. Prick plastic to release steam.
- Remove from oven and uncover. Sprinkle the salt into the broth made by the fish. Serve immediately, spooning the broth over the fish.

Nutrition Information

- 465: calories;
- 1 gram: sugars;
- 2 grams: polyunsaturated fat;
- 3 grams: carbohydrates;
- 0 grams: dietary fiber;
- 93 grams: protein;
- 366 milligrams: sodium;
- 6 grams: fat;

146.   Rhubarb Lamb Stew

Serving: 4 to 5 servings | Prep: | Cook: | Ready in: 24mins

Ingredients

- 1 tablespoon ground cumin
- 1 tablespoon kosher salt
- 1 ½ cups plus 1 tablespoon water
- 14 ounces rhubarb, trimmed and cut on the diagonal in 1/8-inch slices (2 cups)
- 2 pounds boneless leg of lamb, cut in 1 1/4-inch cubes
- 3 medium-size cloves garlic, smashed, peeled and minced
- 1 tablespoon cornstarch

- 1 cup loosely packed cilantro leaves, chopped

Direction

- Stir cumin and salt into 1 1/2 cups of water. Mound rhubarb in the center of a 2 1/2-quart souffle dish with a tight-fitting lid. Pour cumin mixture around rhubarb. Cook, covered, at 100 percent power in a high-power oven for 7 minutes 30 seconds.
- Remove from oven and uncover. Arrange lamb in layers around the inside rim of the dish. Sprinkle garlic over lamb. Re-cover and cook for 5 minutes, stirring once.
- While soup is cooking, stir remaining tablespoon of water into cornstarch. Remove dish from oven and uncover. Stir a few tablespoons of the cooking liquid into the cornstarch mixture. Stir the mixture and the cilantro into soup. Re-cover and cook for 2 minutes.
- Remove from oven and uncover. Ladle into bowls; serve immediately.

Nutrition Information

- 403: calories;
- 34 grams: protein;
- 726 milligrams: sodium;
- 27 grams: fat;
- 11 grams: monounsaturated fat;
- 2 grams: polyunsaturated fat;
- 5 grams: carbohydrates;
- 1 gram: sugars;

147.   Rich Meat Broth

Serving: Three and one-half cups | Prep: | Cook: | Ready in: P2DT45mins

Ingredients

- 1 carrot, peeled and cut into 1-inch pieces, about 3 ounces

- 1 rib celery, cut into 1-inch pieces, about 2 ounces
- 1 leek, cleaned and cut into 1-inch pieces, about 4 ounces
- 2 pounds veal bones, cut into 2-inch pieces
- ½ pound lean beef stew meat, in 2-inch pieces

Direction

- Combine the carrot, celery and leek in a food processor and coarsely chop. Scrape the mixture into a five-quart casserole with a tightly fitting lid. Add the remaining ingredients and four cups of cold water. Cover and cook at 100 percent power in a 650- to 700-watt oven for 30 minutes.
- Remove from the oven and uncover. Strain the broth through a fine sieve. If you wish to skim off the fat, refrigerate the broth so that the fat rises to the surface, then skim with a large spoon. Store, covered, in the refrigerator for up to two days, or freeze.

Nutrition Information

- 28: calories;
- 1 gram: saturated fat;
- 0 grams: sugars;
- 3 grams: protein;
- 32 milligrams: sodium;

---

148. Rich Red Wine Vegetable Stew

Serving: 5 to 6 cups | Prep: | Cook: | Ready in: 1hours35mins

Ingredients

- ¼ cup plus 2 teaspoons vegetable oil
- 2 medium tomatoes, cored
- 1 onion, peeled and cut in half lengthwise
- 2 cups red wine
- 3 garlic cloves, smashed, peeled and chopped
- 1 ounce dried boletus mushrooms, ground in a spice mill
- 1 bay leaf
- 1 ½ tablespoons tomato paste
- ¼ teaspoon dried marjoram
- ¼ teaspoon dried thyme
- 10 ounces fresh mushrooms, cut in1/2-inch pieces
- 5 ½ ounces (1 1/2 cups) green beans, tipped and tailed
- ½ pound turnip, peeled and cut into 1/4-inch thick julienne (1 1/2 cups)
- 3 medium carrots, peeled and cut into 1/4-inch thick julienne (1 1/2 cups)
- Black pepper to taste
- 2 tablespoons cornstarch
- 2 tablespoons water
- 1 bunch parsley, chopped
- 4 teaspoons kosher salt

Direction

- Preheat broiler. Coat tomatoes and onion with 2 teaspoons of oil. Place on a cookie sheet and broil for 12 minutes, turning halfway through.
- Remove from the oven. Coarsely chop tomatoes and onion in a food processor. Reserve.
- While tomatoes and onion broil, place wine, garlic, ground mushrooms and bay leaf in a 5-quart dish with a tightly fitted lid. Cook, uncovered, at 100 percent power in a 650- to 700-watt oven for 15 minutes.
- Remove from oven and uncover. Transfer wine mixture to a small bowl. Whisk in tomato paste, marjoram and thyme. Reserve.
- Place mushrooms in the dish and toss with the remaining 1/4 cup oil. Cook, uncovered, for 10 minutes.
- Remove from oven. Scrape tomato mixture over mushrooms and smooth into an even layer. Arrange green beans in a circle around the outer edge of the dish. Arrange turnips in a circle just inside green beans. Place carrots in the center of the dish. Pour the wine mixture over the vegetables. Sprinkle with pepper. Cook, covered, for 30 minutes.

- Combine cornstarch and water in a small bowl and scrape into dish. Add parsley and stir well. Cook, covered, for 3 minutes.
- Remove from oven. Stir in salt.

Nutrition Information

- 241: calories;
- 741 milligrams: sodium;
- 11 grams: fat;
- 1 gram: saturated fat;
- 2 grams: polyunsaturated fat;
- 0 grams: trans fat;
- 8 grams: sugars;
- 19 grams: carbohydrates;
- 4 grams: protein;

149.   Rich Veal Broth

Serving: 4 cups | Prep: | Cook: | Ready in: 1hours45mins

Ingredients

- 1 large tomato, cored and halved
- 1 large onion, halved
- 1 tablespoon vegetable oil, optional
- 4 cups water
- 2 pounds veal bones, split and cut into 2-inch pieces
- 1 medium-size carrot (about 3 ounces), peeled and diced
- 1 rib celery (about 2 ounces), peeled and diced
- 1 leek (4 ounces), trimmed, rinsed and diced

Direction

- If desired, preheat conventional oven to 450 degrees. Brush tomato and onion with vegetable oil and place in a roasting pan along with the bones. Bake for about 40 minutes, shaking the pan occasionally. Remove from oven and place tomato and onion in a 5-quart casserole with tight-fitting lid. Place roasting pan on top of the stove. Stir 1 cup of the water

into roasting pan to loosen all the brown bits from the bottom, and bring to a boil over moderate heat. Remove from heat and pour mixture into the casserole.
- Combine all remaining ingredients in the casserole. Cook, covered, at 100 percent power in a 650- to 700-watt oven for 40 minutes.
- Remove from oven and uncover. Strain broth through a fine sieve. If not using at once, pour broth into containers and store, covered, in the refrigerator or freezer. If you wish to skim the fat off, refrigerate so the fat rises to the surface and hardens, then remove with a large spoon.

Nutrition Information

- 24: calories;
- 1 gram: carbohydrates;
- 0 grams: sugars;
- 2 grams: protein;
- 45 milligrams: sodium;

150.   Rolled Oats With Amaranth Seeds, Maple Syrup And Apple

Serving: 1 serving | Prep: | Cook: | Ready in: 5mins

Ingredients

- ⅓ cup rolled oats
- 1 tablespoon amaranth seeds
- Generous pinch of salt, or to taste
- 1 tablespoon golden raisins
- 1 teaspoon maple syrup, more for drizzling
- ¼ apple
- Milk and/or chopped toasted walnuts or almonds, for topping (optional)

Direction

- Stir together oats, amaranth seeds, salt and raisins in a medium-size microwave-proof bowl. Bring 2/3 cup water to a boil and pour over mixture. Add maple syrup and stir together, then cover bowl with a plate and leave it out on the counter overnight. (You can refrigerate if you prefer.)

- In the morning, place bowl (still covered by the plate) in the microwave and cook for 2 minutes on 100 percent power. Remove from the microwave and very carefully remove plate from top of bowl. (Bowl will be hot, and steam will rise from cereal.) Stir the mixture. If it is not yet thick, cover again and return to microwave. Cook 1 to 2 minutes longer, until the mixture is no longer watery.
- Transfer to a serving dish. Coarsely grate apple over cereal and stir in. Drizzle on more maple syrup and, if desired, add a little milk, and walnuts or almonds.

Nutrition Information

- 194: calories;
- 3 grams: fat;
- 0 grams: saturated fat;
- 40 grams: carbohydrates;
- 5 grams: dietary fiber;
- 6 grams: protein;
- 217 milligrams: sodium;
- 1 gram: polyunsaturated fat;
- 11 grams: sugars;

---

151.   Sada Chawal (Plain Cooked Basmati Rice)

Serving: Four to six servings | Prep: | Cook: | Ready in: 25mins

Ingredients

- 1 cup Basmati rice

Direction

- Pick the rice clean and wash several times. Drain thoroughly and place in a 2 1/2-quart

microwave-proof dish. Add 2 1/4 cups of water and mix well.

- Cook, uncovered, at 100 percent power in a 650- to 700-watt microwave carousel oven for 8 to 10 minutes, or until most of the water is absorbed and the top of the rice is covered with steamy holes. Stir twice during the cooking time.
- Cover and continue cooking at 100 percent power for 4 minutes, or until the rice is fully cooked and soft. Remove from the oven and set aside, covered, for 5 minutes. Uncover, lightly fluff the rice with a fork and serve.

Nutrition Information

- 113: calories;
- 0 grams: sugars;
- 25 grams: carbohydrates;
- 2 grams: protein;
- 2 milligrams: sodium;

---

152.   Salmon With New Potatoes And Dill

Serving: 2 main-course servings | Prep: | Cook: | Ready in: 20mins

Ingredients

- 2 teaspoons cornstarch
- ½ cup heavy cream
- ½ teaspoon kosher salt
- 2 tablespoons chopped dill
- 1 2-pound coho salmon
- 6 small new potatoes, cut in half
- Freshly ground black pepper to taste

Direction

- Stir the cornstarch and 2 teaspoons of the cream together until smooth. Slowly stir in the remaining cream and the salt. Pour the cream mixture into the bottom of a 14-by-9-by-2-inch oval dish. Place half the dill in the cavity of the salmon. Place the salmon so that it fits against the inside edge of the dish, with the spine side facing out.

- Arrange the potatoes, cut side down, against the opposite edge of the dish. Scatter the remaining dill over the potatoes. Sprinkle pepper over the fish and potatoes. Cover tightly with microwave plastic wrap. Cook at 100 percent power in a high-power oven for 11 minutes. Prick plastic to release steam.
- Remove from oven and uncover. Cover the dish loosely with a kitchen towel for 5 minutes. Uncover and serve immediately, spooning the sauce over the fish.

Nutrition Information

- 1034: calories;
- 104 grams: protein;
- 40 grams: carbohydrates;
- 5 grams: dietary fiber;
- 3 grams: sugars;
- 16 grams: monounsaturated fat;
- 10 grams: polyunsaturated fat;
- 716 milligrams: sodium;
- 49 grams: fat;
- 20 grams: saturated fat;

153. Scallion Soup

Serving: | Prep: | Cook: |Ready in: 38mins

Ingredients

- 1 pound scallions (about 4 bunches or 24 scallions), trimmed and cut across into 1-inch lengths
- 3 ½ cups vegetarian broth (see Micro Tips) or canned chicken broth
- 4 teaspoons cornstarch
- 1 ⅓ teaspoons kosher salt
- ⅛ teaspoon freshly ground black pepper

Direction

- Combine scallions with 1 cup of the broth in a 2 1/2-quart souffle dish or casserole with a lid. Cover tightly with microwave plastic wrap or with lid. Cook at 100 percent power for 12 minutes in a 650- to 700-watt oven. If using plastic, prick to release steam.
- Remove from oven and uncover. Pour mixture into a food processor and puree. Pour back into souffle dish. Dissolve cornstarch in remaining broth and add to scallion mixture. Cover and cook for 8 minutes. If using plastic, prick to release steam.
- Remove from oven. Uncover, stir in salt and pepper and serve.

Nutrition Information

- 119: calories;
- 1 gram: fat;
- 0 grams: polyunsaturated fat;
- 23 grams: carbohydrates;
- 6 grams: dietary fiber;
- 7 grams: protein;
- 1653 milligrams: sodium;

154. Scrod With Clams Livornese

Serving: 4 servings | Prep: | Cook: |Ready in: 17mins

Ingredients

- 1 ½ pounds scrod fillet, 1/2-inch thick
- ¼ cup olive oil
- 3 tablespoons white wine
- kosher salt to taste
- Freshly ground black pepper
- 16 littleneck clams, well scrubbed
- 4 cloves garlic, smashed and peeled

Direction

- Place fish in the center of an oval dish 14 by 9 by 2 inches. Sprinkle with the oil, wine, salt and pepper. Arrange clams, hinge side down, around side of dish. Place garlic between clams.
- Cover tightly with microwave plastic wrap. Cook at 100 percent power in a high-power oven for 12 minutes. Prick plastic to release steam.
- Remove from oven and uncover. Serve hot.

Nutrition Information

- 324: calories;
- 39 grams: protein;
- 596 milligrams: sodium;
- 15 grams: fat;
- 2 grams: polyunsaturated fat;
- 0 grams: sugars;
- 10 grams: monounsaturated fat;
- 4 grams: carbohydrates;

155. Shrimp Creole

Serving: Eight to ten servings | Prep: | Cook: | Ready in: 1hours30mins

Ingredients

- 5 bacon slices
- 5 medium onions, finely diced
- 7 celery stalks, finely diced
- 3 large bell peppers, finely diced
- 1 6-ounce can of tomato paste
- 4 ripe tomatoes, chopped, with juice
- ½ cup sugar
- 3 pounds medium shrimp, deveined and peeled
- 1 tablespoon Worcestershire sauce, plus more to taste
- Salt and pepper to taste

Direction

- In a microwave, cook the bacon for 4 to 5 minutes at full power to render the fat.
- Pour the fat into a large saucepan. Place over medium heat. Add the onion, celery and pepper. Saute for 10 minutes, or until tender.
- Add the tomato paste, tomatoes and sugar. Cook over low heat, covered, for an hour, stirring occasionally.
- Stir in the shrimp and Worcestershire sauce. Season to taste with salt and pepper. Cover and allow to cook for 15 more minutes. Serve with steamed rice and hot biscuits.

Nutrition Information

- 264: calories;
- 27 grams: carbohydrates;
- 18 grams: sugars;
- 23 grams: protein;
- 1047 milligrams: sodium;
- 4 grams: dietary fiber;
- 8 grams: fat;
- 2 grams: saturated fat;
- 0 grams: trans fat;
- 3 grams: monounsaturated fat;
- 1 gram: polyunsaturated fat;

156. Shrimp Gumbo

Serving: Four to six servings | Prep: | Cook: | Ready in: 35mins

Ingredients

- 4 tablespoons butter
- 4 tablespoons flour
- 1 large yellow onion (about 1/2 pound), halved and sliced 1/4-inch thick
- 3 large celery ribs, trimmed, peeled and sliced 1/4-inch thick (about 1 1/2 cups)
- ½ cup coarsely chopped celery leaves
- 10 cloves garlic, smashed and peeled
- ½ teaspoon cayenne pepper
- 2 teaspoons file powder

- 2 cups canned or fresh chicken broth
- ½ pound fresh okra, trimmed but leaving pod intact
- 2 pounds medium shrimp (about 24 per pound), peeled
- 1 tablespoon kosher salt
- 2 tablespoons fresh lemon juice
- Freshly ground black pepper
- ¼ teaspoon red, hot-pepper sauce

Direction

- In a rectangular ceramic dish (11 by 8 by 3 inches), heat the butter, uncovered, at 100 percent for three minutes. Stir in the flour thoroughly. Cook at 100 percent, uncovered, for eight minutes, until dark brown, stirring twice.
- Add the onion, celery, celery leaves, garlic and cayenne pepper, stirring to coat with roux. Cook, uncovered, at 100 percent for five minutes.
- Stir in file powder, broth and okra. Cover tightly with microwave plastic wrap. Cook at 100 percent for six minutes.
- Uncover carefully and stir in the shrimp. Recover tightly and cook at 100 percent for five minutes. Slit the plastic and stir. Patch the plastic and cook for four minutes longer.
- Uncover. Season to taste with salt, lemon juice, pepper and pepper sauce. Serve with white rice.

Nutrition Information

- 270: calories;
- 25 grams: protein;
- 11 grams: fat;
- 0 grams: trans fat;
- 3 grams: dietary fiber;
- 4 grams: sugars;
- 6 grams: saturated fat;
- 1 gram: polyunsaturated fat;
- 19 grams: carbohydrates;
- 1002 milligrams: sodium;

157.   Shrimp Oriental

Serving: 6 servings | Prep: | Cook: | Ready in: 45mins

Ingredients

- 2 tablespoons dark Oriental sesame oil
- 10 cloves garlic, smashed, peeled and quartered lengthwise
- 3 bunches scallions, white part cut in 1-inch pieces; greens cut across thinly to make 1 cup
- 3 medium-size red bell peppers, cut in 1/2-inch pieces
- 2 tablespoons cornstarch
- 3 tablespoons mirin (sweet Japanese wine)
- ¼ cup tamari sauce
- ¼ cup rice-wine vinegar
- ¼ cup peeled and grated fresh ginger
- 1 8-ounce can sliced water chestnuts, drained and rinsed
- 1 pound large shrimp, peeled and deveined
- 1 ounce dried shiitake mushrooms, stemmed and broken into 1/2-inch pieces
- 10 ounces fresh plum tomatoes, cored and cut in 1/2-inch pieces
- 2 bunches fresh coriander, leaves chopped
- Hot pepper sauce to taste
- Coarse salt to taste

Direction

- Combine oil, garlic and white parts of scallions in a 2 1/2-quart dish. Cook at 100 percent power in a 650- to 700-watt oven, uncovered, for 3 minutes.
- Stir in bell peppers. Cook, uncovered, for 2 minutes.
- While peppers are cooking, place cornstarch and mirin in a small bowl and mix well. Stir in tamari sauce, vinegar, ginger and water chestnuts. Reserve.
- Remove dish from oven. Push vegetables toward the center of the dish and arrange shrimp around the vegetables. Place mushrooms over shrimp and vegetables. Place tomatoes over mushrooms. Pour cornstarch

mixture over all. Cover tightly with a lid or microwave plastic wrap. Cook for 3 minutes 30 seconds. Prick plastic to release steam.

- Uncover and stir in coriander and scallion greens. Re-cover and cook for 2 minutes. Prick plastic to release steam.
- Remove from oven. Uncover and stir in pepper mixture and salt.

Nutrition Information

- 219: calories;
- 26 grams: carbohydrates;
- 7 grams: sugars;
- 6 grams: dietary fiber;
- 1 gram: saturated fat;
- 0 grams: trans fat;
- 2 grams: polyunsaturated fat;
- 15 grams: protein;
- 1125 milligrams: sodium;

158.   Shrimp And Corn Curry

Serving: 4 servings (5 cups) | Prep: | Cook: |Ready in: 40mins

Ingredients

- 2 tablespoons vegetable oil, preferably canola
- 3 tablespoons curry powder
- 1 medium onion, chopped
- 1 tablespoon black mustard seeds
- 1 ½ pounds shrimp, peeled and de-veined
- 2 medium tomatoes, cored and chopped
- 2 cups cooked corn kernels (see Micro-Tips)
- 1 tablespoon peeled and grated fresh ginger
- 1 to 2 tablespoons fresh lemon juice
- ¼ cup chopped cilantro
- 1 ½ teaspoons kosher salt
- Freshly ground black pepper to taste

Direction

- Place oil, curry, onion and mustard seeds in a 2 1/2-quart souffle dish with a tightly fitting lid. Cook, uncovered, at 100 percent power in a high-power oven for 4 minutes.
- Stir in shrimp. Cook, covered, for 3 minutes.
- Remove from oven. Stir in tomatoes, corn and ginger. Cook, covered, for 5 minutes.
- Remove from oven. Stir in remaining ingredients.

Nutrition Information

- 326: calories;
- 0 grams: trans fat;
- 3 grams: polyunsaturated fat;
- 29 grams: carbohydrates;
- 28 grams: protein;
- 11 grams: fat;
- 1 gram: saturated fat;
- 973 milligrams: sodium;
- 6 grams: sugars;

159.   Sicilian Salt Cod Stew

Serving: 4 servings (about 5 1/2 cups) | Prep: | Cook: | Ready in: 1hours21mins

Ingredients

- 1 pound salt cod or stockfish
- 2 (8 ounce) baking potatoes, scrubbed
- 12 cups cold water
- ¼ cup olive oil
- 5 cloves garlic, smashed, peeled and minced
- 1 (28 ounce) can Italian plum tomatoes, coarsely chopped with their juice
- ¾ cup oil-cured black olives, pitted and roughly chopped
- ½ cup white wine
- 1 bay leaf
- 1 sprig fresh thyme or 1/8 teaspoon dried
- Pinch sugar
- Freshly ground black pepper to taste
- ⅓ cup golden raisins

- 2 tablespoons pine nuts

Direction

- Rinse salt cod in a sieve under cold running water for 3 minutes. Place the cod in a 2 1/2-quart souffle dish with a tight-fitting lid. Add 4 cups water. Cover with lid and cook in a 650- to 700-watt oven at 100 for 7 minutes. Remove from oven, uncover and rinse the dish in a sieve under cold running water for 3 minutes. Return the fish to the souffle dish and repeat the cooking and rinsing two more times, for a total of three times.
- Prick each potato several times with the point of a knife. Put a double sheet of paper toweling suitable for microwave use on the bottom of the oven. Place potatoes on paper at opposite ends. Cook at 100 percent power in a 650- to 700-watt microwave oven for 11 minutes. Remove from oven; let cool and peel as remaining cooking is done.
- Combine oil and garlic in a 2 1/2-quart souffle dish. Cook, uncovered, at 100 percent power for 2 minutes.
- Remove from oven and stir in tomatoes, olives, white wine, bay leaf, thyme, sugar and pepper. Place pieces of reserved fish in the mixture so that they are covered by the sauce. Cover with lid and cook at 100 percent power for 10 minutes.
- Remove from oven and uncover. Add raisins and pine nuts so that they are just under the surface but do not stir them in. Re-cover with lid and cook at 100 percent power for 5 minutes.
- Remove from oven and uncover. Gently stir together. Slice potatoes across, 1/4-inch thick. Divide potatoes among four large wide bowls. Spoon fish stew over potatoes and serve.

| 160. | Slim Vichyssoise |

Serving: 4 servings | Prep: | Cook: | Ready in: 26mins

Ingredients

- ¾ pound potatoes, peeled and cut into 2-inch chunks
- 2 large leeks (about 1 pound), the white and very light green parts only, cleaned and cut into 2-inch slices
- 2 ½ cups chicken broth
- ⅓ cup part-skim ricotta cheese
- ½ cup buttermilk
- ½ teaspoon kosher salt
- 2 tablespoons snipped fresh chives

Direction

- Put potatoes and leeks in a food processor. Process until coarsely chopped. Scrape into a 2 1/2-quart souffle dish with a tightly fitting lid. Stir in 1 1/2 cups broth. Cook, covered, at 100 percent power in a high-power oven for 16 minutes, stirring once.
- Remove from oven and uncover. Stir in ricotta, buttermilk and salt. Working in batches, puree the mixture in a blender until smooth. (A food processor will not give soup a creamy texture.)
- If serving cold, scrape soup into a bowl and refrigerate until well chilled. If serving hot, scrape mixture back into souffle dish. Cook, covered, 2 minutes. Serve with chives sprinkled on top.

Nutrition Information

- 199: calories;
- 5 grams: fat;
- 1 gram: polyunsaturated fat;
- 29 grams: carbohydrates;
- 540 milligrams: sodium;
- 2 grams: monounsaturated fat;
- 3 grams: dietary fiber;
- 7 grams: sugars;
- 10 grams: protein;

161. South Indian Eggplant Curry

Serving: 4 or more servings | Prep: | Cook: | Ready in: 15mins

Ingredients

- 2 tablespoons canola oil
- 1 tablespoon chickpea flour
- ¼ teaspoon turmeric powder
- Dash of asafetida
- 3 tablespoons unsweetened shredded coconut
- 1 tablespoon grated ginger
- 1 teaspoon salt, plus more to taste
- 2 teaspoons tamarind paste
- 1 large or 2 medium eggplant
- Chopped fresh cilantro leaves for garnish

Direction

- In a bowl, mix oil, chickpea flour, turmeric and asafetida. Heat on high for 90 seconds, stopping to stir halfway through. In another bowl, heat coconut on high for 90 seconds, stirring halfway through. Add coconut, ginger, salt and tamarind to chickpea mixture.
- Rinse and dry eggplant, trim off ends, and cut into 1-inch slices. Score one side of each slice in several places. Spread and press spice mixture into gashes, then put eggplant into a dish. Partly cover (waxed paper works) and heat on high for 6 minutes. Uncover and cook on high for 2 or 3 minutes, until very soft. Garnish with cilantro. Serve hot or warm.

Nutrition Information

- 133: calories;
- 10 grams: fat;
- 3 grams: saturated fat;
- 0 grams: trans fat;
- 5 grams: dietary fiber;
- 11 grams: carbohydrates;
- 355 milligrams: sodium;
- 2 grams: protein;
- 6 grams: sugars;

162. Spicy Corn Relish

Serving: 4 cups | Prep: | Cook: | Ready in: 28mins

Ingredients

- 4 ounces onion (1 small onion), peeled and cut into chunks
- 2 hot peppers, seeded
- 6 cloves garlic, mashed and peeled
- ½ cup tightly packed fresh coriander leaves
- 1 tablespoon tightly packed oregano leaves
- 1 ½ cups fresh corn kernels (from about 3 ears corn), or canned corn niblets
- 1 large red bell pepper (about 8 ounces), stemmed, seeded, ribbed and cut into 1/2-inch dice
- 3 ribs celery, peeled and chopped (about 3/4 cup chopped)
- 1 tablespoon kosher salt
- 1 ½ teaspoons cumin
- ¾ cup white vinegar
- ½ cup dark Mexican beer

Direction

- Bring a large pot of water to a boil, containing two 8-ounce or four 4-ounce canning jars and their lids to sterilize.
- Place onion, peppers, garlic, coriander and oregano in the bowl of a food processor. Process until coarsely chopped. Scrape mixture into a 2 1/2-quart souffle dish. Stir in remaining ingredients. Cover tightly with microwave plastic wrap. Cook at 100 percent power in a 650- to 700-watt oven for 5 minutes.
- Leaving dish in oven, prick plastic to release steam and uncover carefully. Cook, uncovered, at 100 percent power for 3 minutes.
- Remove from oven. Divide between sterilized jars and store, tightly covered and refrigerated, for up to 2 months.

Nutrition Information

- 142: calories;
- 0 grams: polyunsaturated fat;
- 26 grams: carbohydrates;
- 4 grams: protein;
- 6 grams: sugars;
- 625 milligrams: sodium;
- 1 gram: fat;

163.   Spinach And Coriander Sauce

Serving: 3/4 cup plus 2 tablespoons | Prep: | Cook: | Ready in: 10mins

Ingredients

- 1 pound spinach, stemmed and washed
- 2 tablespoons tightly packed coriander leaves
- ½ cup water
- 3 tablespoons olive oil
- ½ teaspoon kosher salt

Direction

- Place spinach leaves in a 14-by-9-by-2-inch oval dish. Cover tightly with microwave plastic wrap. Cook at 100 percent power in a high-power oven for 4 minutes. Prick plastic to release steam.
- Remove from oven and uncover. Let stand until cool enough to handle. Wring out spinach until dry.
- Place spinach, coriander, water, oil and salt in a blender. Blend until very smooth, stopping from time to time to scrape sides of jar. (Done in a food processor, the sauce will not have a silky texture.)

Nutrition Information

- 309: calories;
- 20 grams: monounsaturated fat;
- 11 grams: carbohydrates;

- 1 gram: sugars;
- 872 milligrams: sodium;
- 28 grams: fat;
- 4 grams: saturated fat;
- 3 grams: polyunsaturated fat;
- 7 grams: dietary fiber;
- 9 grams: protein;

164.   Spring Quiche

Serving: 6 to 8 servings | Prep: | Cook: | Ready in: 42mins

Ingredients

- 2 tablespoons unsalted butter
- ½ pound new potatoes, scrubbed and sliced 1/4 inch thick
- ½ pound chanterelles, cleaned and halved lengthwise, or sliced domestic mushrooms
- ½ cup sliced scallion greens
- 1 ½ teaspoons coarse kosher salt
- Freshly ground pepper to taste
- ¼ cup dry bread crumbs
- ¾ cup small peas
- 4 eggs
- 2 egg yolks
- 1 cup milk
- 1 cup heavy cream
- Pinch nutmeg
- 4 ounces Gruyere, grated
- ⅓ cup fresh chervil leaves

Direction

- Preheat broiler. Position rack 6 inches from heat source.
- In a 2-quart oval or 2 1/2-quart round souffle dish, melt butter at 100 percent power for 2 minutes. Stir in potatoes and mushrooms. Cook, uncovered, at 100 percent for 5 minutes. Add scallions, 1/2 teaspoon salt, pepper, bread crumbs and peas. Cook, uncovered, for 5 minutes.

- Whisk together remaining ingredients including 1 teaspoon salt and pepper to taste. Pour over vegetables; stir. Cover tightly with microwave plastic wrap. Cook at 100 percent for 5 minutes. Slash plastic with a sharp knife. Placing wooden spoon through slit, stir thoroughly. Patch split in plastic with small piece of plastic. Cook 5 minutes longer. Prick plastic to release steam. Uncover and cook 2 minutes.
- Brown under broiler. Allow to stand 10 minutes before serving.

Nutrition Information

- 300: calories;
- 13 grams: carbohydrates;
- 4 grams: sugars;
- 2 grams: dietary fiber;
- 12 grams: protein;
- 420 milligrams: sodium;
- 23 grams: fat;
- 0 grams: trans fat;
- 7 grams: monounsaturated fat;

---

165. Spring Stew Of Chicken And Asparagus

Serving: 4 to 6 servings | Prep: | Cook: | Ready in: 18mins

Ingredients

- 6 shallots, peeled and cut crosswise three times
- 1 2 1/2-pound chicken, cut up, backbone and wing tips reserved for broth
- ¾ pound asparagus, trimmed, peeled and cut in 1 1/2 inch pieces, about 2 cups
- 1 cup chicken broth, canned or fresh
- 2 tablespoons cornstarch, dissolved in 1/4 cup cold water
- 2 tablespoons fresh lemon juice
- 2 tablespoons minced fresh dill

- 1 tablespoon kosher salt
- Fresh ground black pepper

Direction

- Scatter shallots in bottom of a 2-quart souffle dish.
- At the knobby, small end of each chicken leg, cut through skin and tendons.
- Arrange legs and thighs along the inside rim of the souffle dish. Place breast halves, bone side up, in center of dish. Fit wings in between legs and thighs. Mound asparagus in center of dish. Pour broth over all. Cover tightly with microwave plastic wrap. Cook at 100 percent for 10 minutes.
- With dish in oven, slit plastic. Stir in dissolved cornstarch by sticking wooden spoon through slit. Cover slit with a square of wrap as a patch. Cook at 100 percent for three minutes.
- Uncover and stir in lemon juice, dill, salt and pepper to taste. Serve immediately

Nutrition Information

- 359: calories;
- 17 grams: carbohydrates;
- 3 grams: dietary fiber;
- 28 grams: protein;
- 4 grams: polyunsaturated fat;
- 824 milligrams: sodium;
- 20 grams: fat;
- 6 grams: sugars;
- 0 grams: trans fat;
- 8 grams: monounsaturated fat;

---

166. Steamed Papaya Pudding

Serving: 8 servings | Prep: | Cook: | Ready in: 30mins

Ingredients

- 1 pound papaya, peeled, seeded and cut into 2-inch pieces

- 1 stick plus 2 tablespoons unsalted butter
- 6 large eggs
- ½ cup sour cream (plus more, if desired, for garnish)
- 6 tablespoons cake flour, sifted
- 1 teaspoon vanilla extract
- 1 teaspoon ground cardamom

Direction

- Place papaya in a 4-cup measuring cup. Cover tightly with plastic wrap. Microwave at 100 percent power for 4 minutes.
- Butter a 9-by-4-inch bowl or a 4-cup souffle dish with 2 tablespoons butter.
- Remove the papaya from the oven. Place in the work bowl of a food processor with remaining ingredients, and blend until smooth.
- Pour batter into the prepared bowl. Cover tightly with plastic wrap. Cook at 100 percent for 9 minutes, until the pudding is set.
- Remove the pudding from oven. Pierce plastic with a sharp knife, and cover the top of the bowl with a heavy plate. Let stand for 15 minutes.
- Unmold the pudding onto a serving plate. Serve warm, with additional sour cream, if desired.

Nutrition Information

- 230: calories;
- 6 grams: protein;
- 60 milligrams: sodium;
- 18 grams: fat;
- 10 grams: saturated fat;
- 1 gram: dietary fiber;
- 5 grams: sugars;
- 12 grams: carbohydrates;

167. Stir Fried Snow Peas With Soba

Serving: Serves four | Prep: | Cook: | Ready in: 10mins

Ingredients

- 1 tablespoon peanut butter (to taste)
- 1 tablespoon soy sauce
- 2 tablespoons white wine vinegar or seasoned rice wine vinegar
- 1 to 2 teaspoons hot red pepper oil (to taste)
- Pinch of cayenne
- Salt
- freshly ground pepper to taste
- 2 large garlic cloves, minced
- 1 tablespoon finely minced fresh ginger
- 1 tablespoon sesame oil
- ½ cup vegetable or chicken broth
- 2 tablespoons canola oil
- ½ pound snow peas, strings and stem ends removed
- 1 bunch scallions, white and light green parts only
- ¼ pound firm tofu, sliced (optional)
- 8 ounces soba noodles, cooked
- 4 large radishes, trimmed, cut in half, and thinly sliced
- 3 tablespoons chopped cilantro

Direction

- Heat the peanut butter for 10 seconds in a microwave to make it easier to mix. Combine with the soy sauce, vinegar, hot red pepper oil, cayenne, half the garlic and ginger, salt and pepper. Whisk together. Whisk in the sesame oil and broth. Set aside.
- Heat the canola or peanut oil in a wok or a large, heavy skillet over medium-high heat, and add the snow peas. Stir-fry for one to two minutes, and add the scallions and remaining garlic and ginger. Stir-fry for 20 seconds, and add the tofu (if using). Stir-fry for one to two minutes, then stir in the noodles and sauce. Toss together until the noodles are hot, and

remove from the heat. Add the radishes and cilantro, stir together, and serve.

Nutrition Information

- 377: calories;
- 2 grams: saturated fat;
- 0 grams: trans fat;
- 8 grams: monounsaturated fat;
- 4 grams: sugars;
- 13 grams: protein;
- 725 milligrams: sodium;
- 15 grams: fat;
- 5 grams: polyunsaturated fat;
- 53 grams: carbohydrates;
- 3 grams: dietary fiber;

---

168.   Striped Bass With Pesto

Serving: 2 main-course servings | Prep: | Cook: | Ready in: 25mins

Ingredients

- 2 ½ cups loosely packed basil leaves
- ½ cup loosely packed Italian parsley leaves
- 12 cloves garlic, smashed and peeled
- ½ cup olive oil
- ½ teaspoon kosher salt
- 1 2-pound striped bass

Direction

- To make the pesto, place basil, parsley, garlic and 2 tablespoons of the olive oil in a food processor. Process until finely chopped. With the machine running, slowly pour in the remaining olive oil. Scrape down sides of bowl, add salt, and process until smooth.
- Using a serrated knife, cut four 2-inch slits across each side of the fish. Place the fish in a 14-by-9-by-2-inch oval dish. It is fine for the tail to hang over the edge of the dish. Rub about half of the pesto all over the fish, into

the slits and inside the cavity. Reserve the remaining pesto to serve with the fish, or pasta if serving, or keep for another use.
- Cover the dish tightly with microwave plastic wrap, making sure the tail is well covered. Cook at 100 percent power in a high-power oven for 11 minutes. Prick plastic to release steam. Remove from oven and uncover. Serve immediately, spooning the liquid over the fish.

Nutrition Information

- 956: calories;
- 797 milligrams: sodium;
- 10 grams: saturated fat;
- 42 grams: monounsaturated fat;
- 9 grams: polyunsaturated fat;
- 1 gram: dietary fiber;
- 0 grams: sugars;
- 65 grams: fat;
- 8 grams: carbohydrates;
- 83 grams: protein;

---

169.   Stuffed Miniature Eggplants

Serving: 8 first-course servings | Prep: | Cook: | Ready in: 38mins

Ingredients

- 4 miniature eggplants (1 pound), cooked as in Micro Tip
- Scant 1/4 cup long-grain white rice
- 1 small onion, peeled and chopped fine (1/3 cup)
- ½ cup loosely packed parsley leaves, chopped fine
- ¼ cup loosely packed fresh mint leaves, chopped fine
- 3 ounces calamata olives (1/2 cup), pitted and coarsely chopped
- ½ cup boxed strained tomatoes, or canned puree

- Grated zest of 1 lemon (about 2 teaspoons)
- 1 tablespoon fresh lemon juice
- 2 tablespoons olive oil
- Scant 1/4 teaspoon ground cinnamon
- 2 teaspoons kosher salt
- Freshly ground black pepper

Direction

- While eggplants are cooking, place rice in a small saucepan with 1/2 cup water. Bring to a boil on the stove. Reduce to a simmer. Cover and cook for 8 minutes, until half cooked. Drain.
- When eggplants are cool enough to handle, cut in half lengthwise. With a small knife, gently scrape out flesh, being careful not to tear the skin. Reserve shells. Coarsely chop flesh.
- In a medium bowl, combine eggplant flesh with rice and remaining ingredients. Divide filling evenly among the eggplant shells.
- Place in a 13-by-9-by-2-inch oval dish. Cover tightly with microwave plastic wrap. Cook at 100 percent power in a high-power oven for 18 minutes. Prick plastic to release steam.
- Remove from oven and uncover. Serve hot or at room temperature.

Nutrition Information

- 79: calories;
- 4 grams: fat;
- 1 gram: protein;
- 3 grams: monounsaturated fat;
- 0 grams: polyunsaturated fat;
- 10 grams: carbohydrates;
- 2 grams: sugars;
- 227 milligrams: sodium;

170.   Stuffed Peppers

Serving: 4 servings | Prep: | Cook: | Ready in: 28mins

Ingredients

- ¼ pound mushrooms, cut into quarters
- ½ pound onion, trimmed, peeled and cut into quarters
- 2 cloves garlic, peeled and smashed
- 1 tablespoon olive oil
- ½ cup packed, coarsely chopped watercress
- ½ cup pastina
- 3 tablespoons water
- 2 red bell peppers, cut in half crosswise and seeded
- Kosher salt (optional)
- Freshly ground black pepper (optional)

Direction

- Place mushrooms, onions and garlic in bowl of food processor. Process until finely chopped.
- Place oil in 9-inch pie plate or quiche dish and add chopped vegetables. Cook, uncovered, at 100 percent for 3 minutes.
- Stir in watercress, pastina and 1 tablespoon water. Fill peppers with stuffing, mounding lightly.
- Arrange peppers, evenly spaced, around edge of pie plate. Pour remaining water in bottom of dish. Sprinkle with salt and pepper. Cover tightly with microwave plastic wrap. Cook at 100 percent for 10 minutes.
- Pierce plastic wrap with the tip of a knife to release steam. Unwrap carefully. Serve within 5 minutes. Also good cold.

Nutrition Information

- 129: calories;
- 4 grams: protein;
- 1 gram: polyunsaturated fat;
- 2 grams: monounsaturated fat;
- 20 grams: carbohydrates;
- 3 grams: dietary fiber;
- 6 grams: sugars;
- 9 milligrams: sodium;

171.   Summer Corn Pudding

Serving: 8 side-dish servings | Prep: | Cook: | Ready in: 15mins

Ingredients

- 2 cups fresh corn kernels (from about 4 ears)
- 3 scallions, trimmed and thinly sliced
- ¼ pound radishes, trimmed and thinly sliced
- 8 ounces small-curd, creamy cottage cheese
- ¾ cup plain yogurt
- ¼ cup heavy cream
- 4 whole large eggs
- 3 egg yolks
- 2 teaspoons kosher salt
- Freshly ground black pepper
- 2 tablespoons chopped fresh dill

Direction

- Toss the corn, scallions and radishes in an 11-by-8-by-2-inch ceramic dish. Cook, uncovered, at 100 percent for five minutes.
- Put the cottage cheese, yogurt, cream, eggs, egg yolks, salt and pepper in a food processor or blender. Blend well. Reserve.
- Sprinkle the dill over the vegetables. Pour the reserved egg mixture over all and stir to combine. Cook, uncovered, at 100 percent for three minutes.
- Whisk thoroughly, being sure to stir up the mixture at the edges of the dish (where it cooks most rapidly). Cook, uncovered, at 100 percent for three minutes.
- Whisk again. Cover tightly with microwave plastic wrap. Cook at 100 percent for two minutes. If not set, cook, covered, for an additional minute. Serve immediately.

Nutrition Information

- 174: calories;
- 4 grams: sugars;
- 0 grams: trans fat;
- 13 grams: carbohydrates;
- 10 grams: protein;

- 342 milligrams: sodium;
- 9 grams: fat;
- 3 grams: monounsaturated fat;
- 1 gram: dietary fiber;

172.   Summer Millet Risotto

Serving: 8 cups | Prep: | Cook: | Ready in: 1hours10mins

Ingredients

- ½ cup olive oil
- 1 medium-size onion, minced
- 2 medium-size garlic cloves, smashed, peeled and minced
- 2 cups millet
- 5 cups chicken broth, or vegetarian broth (see Micro-Tip)
- 2 small zucchini, cut in 1/4-inch dice
- 2 medium-size red bell peppers, cored, deribbed and cut in 1/4-inch dice
- 2 cups loosely packed basil leaves, chopped
- ¾ cup pine nuts
- 2 teaspoons kosher salt
- Freshly ground black pepper

Direction

- Place oil in an oval dish, 14 by 9 by 2 inches. Cook, uncovered, at 100 percent in a high-power oven for 2 minutes. Stir in onion and garlic. Cook for 4 minutes.
- Stir in millet and broth. Cook for 20 minutes. Stir in zucchini and peppers. Cook for 21 minutes. Stir in basil and pine nuts. Cook for 2 minutes.
- Remove from oven. Stir in salt and pepper.

Nutrition Information

- 280: calories;
- 334 milligrams: sodium;
- 2 grams: sugars;
- 29 grams: carbohydrates;

- 4 grams: dietary fiber;
- 6 grams: protein;
- 16 grams: fat;
- 8 grams: monounsaturated fat;
- 5 grams: polyunsaturated fat;

- 11 grams: carbohydrates;
- 3 grams: protein;
- 606 milligrams: sodium;
- 7 grams: fat;
- 1 gram: polyunsaturated fat;

173. Summer Squash Medley

Serving: 4 servings | Prep: | Cook: | Ready in: 25mins

Ingredients

- 2 tablespoons olive oil
- 4 to 5 cloves garlic, smashed, peeled and chopped
- 1 ½ medium-size zucchini (3/4 pound), trimmed, quartered lengthwise and cut across into 1/2-inch pieces
- 1 medium-size yellow squash (6 1/2 ounces), trimmed, quartered lengthwise, seeded and cut across into 1/2-inch pieces
- 2 large tomatoes (8 ounces each), cored and cut in 1-inch chunks
- 1 tablespoon kosher salt
- 1 cup basil leaves, coarsely chopped

Direction

- Put oil in a 2 1/2-quart souffle dish with a tightly fitting lid. Cook, uncovered, at 100 percent power in a high-power oven for 1 minute. Stir in garlic. Cook, uncovered, 1 minute 30 seconds.
- Stir in squash. Cook, covered, 5 minutes.
- Uncover and stir in tomatoes and salt. Cook, uncovered, 6 minutes. Stir in basil and cook, uncovered, 1 minute.
- Remove from oven. Let stand, covered, 5 minutes.

Nutrition Information

- 112: calories;
- 5 grams: sugars;

174. Summer Vegetable Stew

Serving: 4 cups; 4 servings as a main course, 8 as a side dish | Prep: | Cook: | Ready in: 36mins

Ingredients

- ½ pound small new potatoes, scrubbed and cut into quarters
- ¼ cup water
- 6 ounces baby carrots, about 10 very small ones, peeled and cut in half crosswise
- 3 cloves garlic, smashed, peeled and sliced
- 10 ounces asparagus, ends snapped off, cut into 1-inch pieces
- 6 ounces plum tomatoes, cored and cut into 1/2-inch chunks
- 6 ounces small zucchini, trimmed and cut into 1/4-inch slices
- 2 ounces small peas, fresh or frozen (defrosted in a sieve under warm running water)
- 2 ounces corn kernels, fresh or frozen (defrosted in a sieve under warm running water)
- 3 tablespoons unsalted butter
- ½ cup basil leaves, shredded
- 1 teaspoon kosher salt
- Freshly ground black pepper to taste

Direction

- Place potatoes and water in a 2 1/2-quart souffle dish or casserole with tight-fitting lid. Cook, covered, at 100 percent power in a 650- to 700-watt oven for 3 minutes.
- Remove from oven and uncover. Stir in carrots and garlic. Re-cover and cook for 3 minutes.
- Remove from oven and uncover. Top with asparagus. Re-cover and cook for 2 minutes.

- Remove from oven and uncover. Add tomatoes in a single layer and place zucchini slices over tomatoes. Re-cover and cook for 6 minutes, stirring once during cooking.
- Remove from oven and uncover. Top with peas, corn and butter. Re-cover and cook for 2 minutes.
- Remove from oven and uncover. Stir in remaining ingredients; serve.

Nutrition Information

- 200: calories;
- 6 grams: protein;
- 1 gram: polyunsaturated fat;
- 26 grams: carbohydrates;
- 7 grams: sugars;
- 518 milligrams: sodium;
- 9 grams: fat;
- 0 grams: trans fat;
- 2 grams: monounsaturated fat;

175.   Supernatural Brownies

Serving: 15 large or 24 small brownies | Prep: | Cook: | Ready in: 1hours

Ingredients

- 2 sticks (16 tablespoons) butter, more for pan and parchment paper
- 8 ounces bittersweet chocolate
- 1 cup dark brown sugar, such as muscovado
- 1 cup granulated sugar
- 4 eggs
- ½ teaspoon salt
- 2 teaspoons vanilla extract
- 1 cup flour
- ½ cup chopped walnuts or 3/4 cup whole walnuts, optional

Direction

- Butter a 13-by-9-inch baking pan and line with buttered parchment paper. Preheat oven to 350 degrees. In top of a double boiler set over barely simmering water, or on low power in a microwave, melt butter, chocolate and sugars together. Cool slightly. In a large bowl or mixer, whisk eggs. Whisk in salt and vanilla.
- Whisk in chocolate mixture. Fold in flour just until combined. If using chopped walnuts, stir them in. Pour batter into prepared pan. If using whole walnuts, arrange on top of batter. Bake for 35 to 40 minutes or until shiny and beginning to crack on top. Cool in pan on rack.

Nutrition Information

- 318: calories;
- 18 grams: fat;
- 39 grams: carbohydrates;
- 31 grams: sugars;
- 3 grams: protein;
- 100 milligrams: sodium;
- 11 grams: saturated fat;
- 1 gram: dietary fiber;
- 5 grams: monounsaturated fat;

176.   Sweet Custard

Serving: 4 servings | Prep: | Cook: | Ready in: 5mins

Ingredients

- 1 ¼ cups milk
- 1 2-inch piece vanilla bean
- 4 large eggs
- ¼ cup granulated sugar

Direction

- Combine milk and vanilla bean in glass measure. Cook, uncovered, at 100 percent power (see chart). Remove vanilla bean.
- Whisk together eggs and sugar. Whisking constantly but not vigorously, pour hot milk

into eggs. Divide among 4 or 2 custard cups and skim any foam from tops. Cook, uncovered for time given in chart, or until set.

- Remove from oven and let stand until cool. Serve at room temperature or chilled.

Nutrition Information

- 170: calories;
- 9 grams: protein;
- 17 grams: sugars;
- 0 grams: trans fat;
- 2 grams: monounsaturated fat;
- 1 gram: polyunsaturated fat;
- 104 milligrams: sodium;
- 7 grams: fat;
- 3 grams: saturated fat;

---

177.   Sweet Potato Gratin

Serving: 8 servings | Prep: | Cook: | Ready in: 37mins

Ingredients

- 4 large cooked sweet potatoes (about 8 ounces each), peeled and cut into 1/4-inch slices
- 8 ounces grated Gruyere cheese
- 2 cloves garlic, peeled, smashed and minced
- 1 cup heavy cream
- Pinch nutmeg
- Kosher salt, to taste
- Freshly ground black pepper, to taste

Direction

- Place about a third of the potato slices in one layer over the base of a glass or ceramic dish (8 by 8 by 2 inches). Sprinkle a third of the grated cheese and half of the garlic over the potatoes. Cover with another layer of the potato slices, another third of the cheese and the remaining garlic. Top with the remaining potato slices. Reserve the remaining cheese.

- In a small bowl stir together the cream, nutmeg, salt and pepper. Pour mixture over the potatoes. Cover tightly with microwavable plastic wrap.
- Cook at 100 percent power in a 650-to-700-watt oven for 6 minutes.
- Preheat conventional broiler.
- Prick plastic to release steam, remove from oven and uncover. Sprinkle the reserved cheese over the potatoes. Place under the broiler for a few minutes, until browned.
- Remove from broiler and allow to stand for a few minutes before serving.

Nutrition Information

- 292: calories;
- 18 grams: carbohydrates;
- 402 milligrams: sodium;
- 20 grams: fat;
- 12 grams: saturated fat;
- 6 grams: monounsaturated fat;
- 1 gram: polyunsaturated fat;
- 3 grams: dietary fiber;
- 4 grams: sugars;
- 10 grams: protein;

---

178.   Sweet Potato Ice Cream

Serving: About 3 cups ice cream | Prep: | Cook: | Ready in: 2hours15mins

Ingredients

- 2 large sweet potatoes, scrubbed
- 1 cup milk
- 4 egg yolks, from large eggs
- ⅔ cup firmly packed light brown sugar
- Pinch salt
- 1 teaspoon ground cinnamon
- ½ teaspoon ground ginger
- 1 teaspoon ground nutmeg
- 1 cup heavy cream
- ⅛ teaspoon vanilla extract

- 1 cup coarsely chopped pecans or black walnuts, optional

Direction

- Preheat oven to 400 degrees.
- Prick the sweet potatoes all over with a fork. Place on a baking sheet and bake 40 to 60 minutes, or until very soft. (To cook the potatoes in a microwave oven, prick, wrap in paper towels, and cook on high 5 to 8 minutes, or until soft, turning once. Remove paper towel, wrap potatoes in foil, and let stand 3 to 5 minutes. Proceed as directed.) Cool until easy to handle, then remove and discard the peel. Puree the flesh in a food processor or blender, then press through a sieve. Measure out 1 cup puree (use any excess for making sweet potato pasta, or to add to soups or stews) and set aside.
- In a small saucepan, scald milk and set aside.
- In a bowl, beat egg yolks well. Beat in sugar, salt and spices. Add hot milk slowly, whisking constantly. Pour mixture into the top of a double boiler and cook over barely simmering water, stirring constantly, 5 to 8 minutes or until mixture coats the back of a spoon.
- Turn off the heat, whisk in the potato puree. Cool to room temperature; stir in cream and vanilla. Chill in the refrigerator for at least 1 hour. Freeze in an ice-cream maker according to manufacturer's directions. Fold in nuts, if desired.

Nutrition Information

- 250: calories;
- 14 grams: fat;
- 4 grams: monounsaturated fat;
- 92 milligrams: sodium;
- 8 grams: saturated fat;
- 1 gram: dietary fiber;
- 29 grams: carbohydrates;
- 22 grams: sugars;
- 3 grams: protein;

179. Swordfish With Tomatoes

Serving: 8 servings | Prep: | Cook: | Ready in: 25mins

Ingredients

- 4 large tomatoes, cored and coarsely chopped (about 4 cups)
- 1 cup fresh basil leaves (loosely packed), cut across into thin strips
- 2 tablespoons olive oil
- 1 tablespoon fresh lemon juice
- Kosher salt and freshly ground black pepper, to taste
- 3 pounds swordfish steak, cut into 8 pieces about 1 inch thick

Direction

- Combine all ingredients except swordfish in a glass or ceramic dish (14 by 11 by 2 inches). Cover tightly with microwave plastic wrap. Cook at 100 percent power in a 650- to 700-watt oven for 4 minutes. Prick plastic to release steam.
- Remove from oven, uncover and stir well. Arrange pieces of fish in the dish so that the skin is toward the edge of the dish. Spoon some of the tomatoes over the fish. Cover tightly with microwave plastic wrap. Cook at 100 percent power for 10 minutes. Prick plastic to release steam.
- Remove from oven and uncover. With a large spatula pile fish on a platter and allow to stand, loosely covered for about 3 minutes. Meanwhile transfer tomato mixture to a blender and process until smooth.
- Serve sauce over fish.

180. Thai Chicken Satay

Serving: 1 serving | Prep: | Cook: | Ready in: 5mins

Ingredients

- For the sauce:
- ¼ cup crunchy peanut butter (preferably natural, unsweetened)
- 2 tablespoons sesame oil
- 1 tablespoon soy sauce
- 1 tablespoon honey
- 1 teaspoon milk
- For the satay:
- 1 cooked chicken breast
- 2 tablespoons soy sauce
- 2 tablespoons honey
- 1 teaspoon sesame seeds

Direction

-
-

Nutrition Information

- 949: calories;
- 4 grams: dietary fiber;
- 59 grams: sugars;
- 35 grams: protein;
- 2691 milligrams: sodium;
- 64 grams: fat;
- 11 grams: saturated fat;
- 0 grams: trans fat;
- 29 grams: monounsaturated fat;
- 21 grams: polyunsaturated fat;
- 70 grams: carbohydrates;

181. Tomato Puree (Basic Tomato Sauce)

Serving: 2 cups | Prep: | Cook: | Ready in: 37mins

Ingredients

- 2 ½ pounds tomatoes

Direction

- Core tomatoes. Cut a slit in the skin of each. Place in a 2 1/2-quart souffle dish and cover tightly with microwave plastic wrap. Cook in a 650-to 700-watt oven at 100 percent power for 12 minutes. Prick plastic with the tip of a sharp knife to release steam. Remove from oven and uncover carefully.
- Pass tomatoes through the medium disc of a food mill. Return tomato puree to dish and cook, uncovered, at 100 percent power for 20 minutes, stirring once or twice, until puree is reduced by half.
- Remove from oven and use, or let cool to room temperature and refrigerate or freeze in 1-cup or 1/2-cup quantities in microwavable storage containers.

Nutrition Information

- 51: calories;
- 1 gram: fat;
- 0 grams: polyunsaturated fat;
- 11 grams: carbohydrates;
- 3 grams: dietary fiber;
- 7 grams: sugars;
- 2 grams: protein;
- 14 milligrams: sodium;

182. Tomato Sauce Casalinga

Serving: 8 servings | Prep: | Cook: | Ready in: 30mins

Ingredients

- 1 small onion, peeled and finely chopped
- 1 small carrot, peeled and finely chopped
- 1 small rib celery, peeled and finely chopped
- 2 medium mushrooms, trimmed and thinly sliced
- 3 ½ cups plum tomato sauce (see Micro-Tip)
- 1 teaspoon chopped fresh oregano
- 2 teaspoons chopped fresh basil
- 1 tablespoon fresh lemon juice
- 1 ½ teaspoons kosher salt

- Pinch ground black pepper

Direction

- Combine onion, carrot, celery and mushrooms in a 2 1/2-quart souffle dish. Cover with a paper towel. Cook at 100 percent power in a high-power oven for 5 minutes.
- Stir in tomato sauce and oregano. Cook, uncovered, for 13 minutes, stirring once. Stir in basil. Cook for 2 minutes.
- Remove from oven and uncover. Stir in lemon juice, salt and pepper.

Nutrition Information

- 34: calories;
- 5 grams: sugars;
- 516 milligrams: sodium;
- 0 grams: polyunsaturated fat;
- 8 grams: carbohydrates;
- 2 grams: protein;

---

183.   Tomato Bluefish Pasta

Serving: | Prep: | Cook: | Ready in: 24mins

Ingredients

- ¾ pound spaghetti
- ½ pound fresh fennel
- ¼ cup olive oil
- ½ yellow onion, peeled and cut into 1 inch wedges
- 6 cloves garlic, peeled and mashed
- 2 cups lightly cooked crushed tomatoes (see recipe) or 2 cups canned crushed tomatoes in juice, drained
- 2 tablespoons capers, drained
- Freshly ground black pepper
- 4 bluefish fillets, 4 ounces each
- 1 ½ tablespoons fresh lemon juice
- Kosher salt

Direction

- On the stove, bring a large pot of salted water to boil.
- Trim fennel by removing the feathery tops. Chop tops finely and reserve. Cut fennel bulb in half through the core. Slice each half through the core into 4 wedges.
- In a glass or ceramic oval dish (11 by 9 by 2 inches), stir fennel, olive oil, onion and garlic until vegetables are coated with oil. Push vegetables to the sides of the dish, leaving the center empty. Cook, uncovered, at 100 percent for 4 minutes.
- Add the spaghetti to the boiling water.
- Pour tomatoes into the center of the dish of vegetables. Sprinkle reserved fennel tops and capers over tomatoes. Sprinkle a small amount of black pepper on top. Cover tightly with microwave plastic wrap. Cook at 100 percent for 5 minutes.
- Carefully uncover the dish. Arrange fish fillets spoke-fashion over tomatoes and vegetables. Cover tightly with microwave plastic wrap. Cook at 100 percent for 5 minutes.
- When pasta is cooked, remove 1/2 cup of the cooking water and pour it into a large bowl. Drain the pasta and add it to the bowl. Gently set the fish fillets on top of the pasta, arranging them around the sides of the bowl. Place vegetables in the center.
- Taste the tomato sauce and season with lemon juice and salt, if desired. Pour sauce over all. Work a small wooden spoon down into the spaghetti in several places so some of the tomato sauce trickles down. Serve immediately.

Nutrition Information

- 260: calories;
- 3 grams: dietary fiber;
- 15 grams: protein;
- 4 grams: sugars;
- 391 milligrams: sodium;
- 8 grams: fat;

- 1 gram: polyunsaturated fat;
- 5 grams: monounsaturated fat;
- 32 grams: carbohydrates;

- 4 grams: dietary fiber;
- 5 grams: sugars;
- 1 gram: protein;

184. Tomato Cranberry Salsa

Serving: 2 1/4 cups | Prep: | Cook: | Ready in: 12mins

Ingredients

- 8 ounces fresh cranberries (2 cups)
- 1 small red onion, peeled and coarsely chopped (1/2 cup)
- ¾ pound ripe tomatoes, cored, seeded and cut in 1/2-inch dice (about 1 3/4 cups), or 3/4 cup canned tomatoes, drained well and coarsely chopped
- 1 fresh jalapeno, seeded, deribbed and coarsely chopped, or 1 canned jalapeno, rinsed, drained and coarsely chopped
- 2 tablespoons fresh lemon juice
- 2 teaspoons Kosher salt
- ½ teaspoon ground cumin

Direction

- Place cranberries and onion in a food processor. Pulse until coarsely chopped. Add tomato and jalapeno. Pulse 2 to 3 times in short bursts just to combine.
- Scrape mixture into a 2 1/2-quart souffle dish. Cover with a lid or microwave plastic wrap. Cook at 100 percent power in a high-power oven for 5 minutes. Prick plastic, if using, to release steam.
- Remove from oven and uncover. Stir in lemon juice, salt and cumin. Let stand until cool.

Nutrition Information

- 44: calories;
- 347 milligrams: sodium;
- 0 grams: polyunsaturated fat;
- 11 grams: carbohydrates;

185. Tomato Vegetable Sauce

Serving: 3 1/2 cups, enough for 3 pounds of dry pasta | Prep: | Cook: | Ready in: 23mins

Ingredients

- 6 cloves garlic, smashed and peeled
- 2 ribs celery, strung and cut into 2-inch pieces
- ¼ pound onion, peeled and quartered
- 1 medium-size red bell pepper, cored, seeded, deribbed and cut in large chunks
- 3 sprigs parsley, stems discarded
- ¼ cup olive oil
- 1 14 1/2-ounce can whole tomatoes in juice, or 1 1/2 cups homemade tomato puree (see recipe)
- 1 tablespoon sweet paprika
- 1 teaspoon hot paprika or chili powder (without cumin)
- 1 ½ teaspoons coarse kosher salt
- ½ cup heavy cream

Direction

- In a food processor, finely chop garlic, celery, onion, red pepper and parsley. In a 2-quart souffle dish, combine chopped vegetables with olive oil. Cook, uncovered, in a 650- to 700-watt oven at 100 percent power for 4 minutes, stirring once.
- While vegetables are cooking, coarsely chop tomatoes in liquid in food processor. Add to chopped vegetables along with seasonings. Cook, uncovered, at 10 percent power for 7 minutes, stirring twice.
- Stir in heavy cream. Taste and adjust seasoning. Serve with spaghettini or linguine.

Nutrition Information

- 158: calories;
- 5 grams: saturated fat;
- 8 grams: monounsaturated fat;
- 2 grams: protein;
- 4 grams: sugars;
- 14 grams: fat;
- 308 milligrams: sodium;
- 1 gram: polyunsaturated fat;
- 7 grams: carbohydrates;

186.   Tostadas With Smashed Black Beans Or Vaqueros

Serving: 8 tostadas, serving 4 to 8 | Prep: | Cook: | Ready in: 45mins

Ingredients

- 1 tablespoon grape seed oil or canola oil
- 2 teaspoons cumin seeds, ground
- 4 cups simmered black beans or vaquero beans, with liquid
- 8 corn tortillas
- ¾ pound ripe tomatoes, finely chopped
- 1 to 2 serrano or jalapeño chiles (to taste), minced
- 2 slices red or white onion, finely chopped and soaked for 5 minutes in water to cover, then drained, rinsed, and drained on paper towels
- ¼ cup chopped cilantro (more to taste)
- 1 teaspoon fresh lime juice (optional)
- 1 small ripe Hass avocado, cut in small dice

Direction

- Heat oil over medium heat in a large, heavy pan (I use a heavy nonstick pan for this) and add cumin. When it is sizzling, add beans with their liquid and turn up heat to medium-high. Cook beans, mashing with the back of your spoon and stirring often, until they are thick but still fairly moist, about 10 to 15 minutes. Remove from heat. Every so often a layer of thick broth should begin to stick to the pan. Stir that into the beans – it has a lot of flavor.

The smashed beans will continue to dry even after you remove from the heat.

- Toast the tortillas. For really crisp tortillas, heat one at a time (2 if you have a large enough microwave to fit 2 without the tortillas overlapping) in a microwave for 1 minute on full power. Flip tortilla over and microwave for 30 seconds to a minute more on full power, until crisp. You can also toast them in a dry pan or directly over the flame, but this will not crisp the tortillas, it will just char them.
- In a medium bowl, combine tomatoes, chiles, onion, and cilantro. Season to taste with salt. Stir in lime juice and the avocado. Let sit for 15 to 30 minutes for the best flavor.
- Spread about 1/2 cup of the refried beans over each tortilla. Top with a generous spoonful of salsa. Place a handful of shredded lettuce or cabbage on top and if desired a little more salsa on the lettuce. Sprinkle on some white cheese, and serve.

Nutrition Information

- 181: calories;
- 9 grams: fat;
- 5 grams: sugars;
- 1 gram: saturated fat;
- 4 grams: protein;
- 3 grams: polyunsaturated fat;
- 25 grams: carbohydrates;
- 7 grams: dietary fiber;
- 25 milligrams: sodium;

187.   Tostadas With Sweet And Hot Peppers And Eggs

Serving: 4 servings | Prep: | Cook: | Ready in: 30mins

Ingredients

- 1 small white onion or 1 bunch scallions, chopped
- 2 large red bell peppers, chopped

- 1 serrano or jalapeño pepper, seeded and minced (more to taste)
- 1 large garlic clove, minced
- ½ pound tomatoes, cut into small dice, or 1 cup canned diced tomatoes, drained
- 3 to 4 tablespoons chopped cilantro
- Salt to taste
- 6 to 8 eggs
- 6 to 8 corn tortillas, cut in half and toasted in the microwave
- 1 cup thinly shredded cabbage (green or red) or romaine lettuce
- Crumbled queso fresco or feta (optional)

Direction

- Heat the oil over medium heat in a large nonstick skillet and add the onion or scallions. Cook, stirring, until tender, about 5 minutes for onion, 2 to 3 for scallions, and add the peppers, chili and garlic. Stir together until the garlic begins to smell fragrant, about 30 seconds, and add salt to taste. Continue to cook, stirring often, until the peppers are quite soft, about 8 minutes. Add the tomatoes and cook, stirring often, until the tomatoes have cooked down and are no longer watery, 8 to 10 minutes.
- Beat the eggs in a bowl, season with salt and pepper, and add to the pepper mixture. Stir in the cilantro and cook, stirring over low heat, until the eggs are just set but still creamy. Remove from the heat and spoon onto the toasted tortillas. Top with shredded cabbage or lettuce, sprinkle with cheese if desired and serve.

Nutrition Information

- 246: calories;
- 3 grams: monounsaturated fat;
- 6 grams: dietary fiber;
- 7 grams: sugars;
- 14 grams: protein;
- 9 grams: fat;
- 0 grams: trans fat;
- 2 grams: polyunsaturated fat;

- 29 grams: carbohydrates;
- 680 milligrams: sodium;

188. Tuna Casserole

Serving: 6 servings | Prep: | Cook: | Ready in: 1hours

Ingredients

- ½ pound fusilli
- 2 medium onions, roughly chopped
- 1 cup celery, chopped
- 3 6-ounce cans of oil-packed tuna, drained
- ⅓ cup prepared horseradish
- ⅓ cup canned or fresh mushrooms, chopped
- 2 cans (10 ounces each) of condensed cream of celery or cream of mushroom soup
- ½ teaspoon garlic powder
- Black pepper to taste
- 1 cup sharp Cheddar cheese, grated
- 1 ½ cups potato chips, crushed

Direction

- Preheat the oven to 350 degrees. Cook the fusilli in well-salted water until al dente and drain.
- Combine the onions and celery with 2 tablespoons of water and microwave about 7 minutes, until the vegetables are soft.
- In a large bowl, combine the tuna, horseradish, mushrooms, condensed soup, garlic powder and the onions and celery. Add the pasta and black pepper to taste and mix thoroughly. Pour into a 1 1/2-quart casserole. Top with the grated Cheddar, and then the chips.
- Bake for 35 to 40 minutes, until the contents are bubbling and the chips are golden brown.

Nutrition Information

- 554: calories;
- 1268 milligrams: sodium;
- 8 grams: monounsaturated fat;

- 48 grams: carbohydrates;
- 6 grams: saturated fat;
- 0 grams: trans fat;
- 7 grams: polyunsaturated fat;
- 4 grams: sugars;
- 37 grams: protein;
- 23 grams: fat;

---

189.   Tuna With Tomatoes

Serving: 4 servings | Prep: | Cook: | Ready in: 15mins

Ingredients

- 6 canned plum tomatoes, drained, squeezed and coarsely chopped
- 1 ½ pounds tuna steak, 1-inch thick
- 1 teaspoon olive oil
- 1 teaspoon fresh lemon juice
- kosher salt to taste
- Freshly ground black pepper to taste
- 6 large basil leaves

Direction

- Spread the tomatoes evenly in an oval dish 13 by 9 by 2 inches. Arrange fish over tomatoes. Drizzle with the oil and lemon juice, and sprinkle with salt and pepper. Scatter basil over all.
- Cover tightly with microwave plastic wrap. Cook at 100 percent power in a high-power oven for 7 1/2 minutes. Prick plastic to release steam.
- Remove from oven. Let stand, covered, for 2 minutes. Uncover and serve immediately.

Nutrition Information

- 215: calories;
- 2 grams: sugars;
- 0 grams: polyunsaturated fat;
- 1 gram: dietary fiber;
- 4 grams: carbohydrates;

- 42 grams: protein;
- 621 milligrams: sodium;

---

190.   Turkey Pate

Serving: 1 8-by-4-inch loaf; makes 36 thin slices or 144 canapes | Prep: | Cook: | Ready in: 20mins

Ingredients

- 2 pounds raw ground turkey or turkey breasts
- 2 scallions, cut in 1-inch pieces
- ¾ cup loosely packed parsley leaves
- ½ cup chicken broth
- 2 tablespoons heavy cream
- ½ teaspoon dried summer savory or 2 teaspoons chopped fresh tarragon
- 2 teaspoons kosher salt
- Freshly ground black pepper to taste
- Vegetable oil for greasing pan

Direction

- If using whole turkey breasts, place in food processor and process until coarsely ground. Reserve ground turkey. Place scallions and parsley in processor and process until coarsely chopped. Add ground turkey and remaining ingredients. Process until smooth.
- Scrape mixture into an oiled loaf pan, 9 by 5 by 3 inches. Cover tightly with microwave plastic wrap. Cook at 100 percent power in a high-power oven (see Micro Tip) for 12 minutes. Prick plastic to release steam.
- Remove from oven. Uncover. Cover with a towel for 10 minutes. Uncover and let stand until cool. Wrap pan tightly with foil or plastic wrap and weight the pate. Refrigerate for 8 to 12 hours. Uncover and unmold onto a plate. Cut into 1/8-inch slices.

Nutrition Information

- 46: calories;
- 3 grams: fat;

- 1 gram: polyunsaturated fat;
- 0 grams: sugars;
- 5 grams: protein;
- 74 milligrams: sodium;

---

191.   Turkey Stew

Serving: 4 servings | Prep: | Cook: | Ready in: 20mins

Ingredients

- 6 ounces frozen pearl onions, defrosted under warm running water
- 4 ounces frozen peas, defrosted under warm running water
- 4 ounces cranberries (1 cup)
- 1 rib celery, peeled and cut across into thin slices (about 1/2 cup)
- 1 cup turkey or chicken broth
- ½ teaspoon dried sage
- ½ teaspoon dried thyme
- 1 pound leftover sliced turkey or turkey cutlets, cut into 1 1/2-inch pieces
- 1 ½ tablespoons cornstarch
- Freshly ground black pepper to taste
- Kosher salt to taste

Direction

- In a 2 1/2-quart souffle dish with a tight-fitting lid, stir together pearl onions, peas, cranberries, celery, turkey or chicken broth, sage and thyme. Cook, covered, at 100 percent power in a high-power oven for 3 minutes.
- Remove from oven and uncover. Stir in turkey pieces. Re-cover and cook for 4 minutes longer, stirring once after first 2 minutes.
- Remove from oven and uncover. Place cornstarch and pepper in a small bowl. Stir in about 1/2 cup of the cooking liquid until no lumps remain. Stir mixture into the stew. Re-cover and cook for 3 minutes.
- Remove from oven and uncover. Stir in salt to taste.

Nutrition Information

- 267: calories;
- 9 grams: fat;
- 3 grams: monounsaturated fat;
- 17 grams: carbohydrates;
- 4 grams: dietary fiber;
- 29 grams: protein;
- 671 milligrams: sodium;
- 2 grams: polyunsaturated fat;
- 5 grams: sugars;

---

192.   Veal Savarin

Serving: 2 servings | Prep: | Cook: | Ready in: 17mins

Ingredients

- ¼ pound mushrooms, trimmed and quartered
- 2 tablespoons parsley leaves, preferably Italian flat leaf
- 4 shallots, peeled
- ½ teaspoon fresh lemon juice
- ½ pound ground veal
- 1 ½ teaspoons kosher salt
- ½ teaspoon paprika
- Freshly ground black pepper to taste
- 2 carrots (5 to 6 ounces), scraped and thinly sliced on the diagonal or julienned

Direction

- Put mushrooms, parsley, shallots and lemon juice in the bowl of a food processor. Process, by pulsing on and off, until finely chopped.
- Scrape chopped vegetables into a mixing bowl. Add ground veal, salt, paprika and pepper. Stir well to combine.
- Divide mixture in half and shape into two doughnuts. Place each in the center of a dinner plate. Arrange carrots around veal. Cover tightly with microwave plastic wrap. Using a rack, cook simultaneously for 5 minutes, switching plates from top to bottom after 2 minutes 30 seconds.

- Pierce plastic on each plate with the tip of a knife to release steam. Uncover and serve immediately.

Nutrition Information

- 356: calories;
- 1 gram: polyunsaturated fat;
- 30 grams: carbohydrates;
- 868 milligrams: sodium;
- 14 grams: sugars;
- 27 grams: protein;
- 15 grams: fat;
- 6 grams: saturated fat;
- 7 grams: dietary fiber;

193. Veal In Tarragon Mushroom Sauce

Serving: 2 servings | Prep: | Cook: | Ready in: 25mins

Ingredients

- 1 ounce dried porcini mushrooms
- 1 small shallot, peeled and thinly sliced across
- ⅔ cup chicken broth
- 2 tablespoons vermouth
- 2 teaspoons cornstarch
- 2 teaspoons water
- 10 ½ ounces boneless loin of veal, cut in 2 1 1/4-inch-thick medallions
- ½ cup frozen baby peas, defrosted in a sieve under warm running water
- 1 tablespoon fresh tarragon leaves
- 4 ounces medium egg noodles
- 1 tablespoon unsalted butter
- Salt and freshly ground black pepper to taste

Direction

- Place mushrooms, shallot and broth in a 2 1/2-quart souffle dish with a tightly fitting lid. Cook, covered, at 100 percent power in a high-power oven for 5 minutes. Remove from oven

and uncover. Stir in vermouth. Stir cornstarch and water together in a small dish. Stir into mushroom mixture. Let stand until cool. Dish can be prepared several hours ahead up to this point. Do not refrigerate.
- Nestle the veal into the sauce, with each medallion against the edge of the dish. Sprinkle the peas around the veal. Scatter the tarragon over all. Cook, covered, at 50 percent power for 12 minutes 30 seconds. Meanwhile, cook noodles. Drain and return them to the pan. Toss with butter and keep warm. Remove veal from oven and uncover. Season with salt and pepper. Serve over noodles.

Nutrition Information

- 675: calories;
- 25 grams: fat;
- 10 grams: monounsaturated fat;
- 1 gram: trans fat;
- 2 grams: polyunsaturated fat;
- 66 grams: carbohydrates;
- 6 grams: sugars;
- 918 milligrams: sodium;
- 7 grams: dietary fiber;
- 44 grams: protein;

194. Vegetable Soup

Serving: | Prep: | Cook: | Ready in: 15mins

Ingredients

- 1 pound chopped zucchini
- 1 ear of corn
- 2 tomatoes, chopped
- 1 tablespoon garlic, slivered
- Splash of stock
- Salt and pepper
- Olive oil, for garnish
- Basil, for garnish

Direction

- Put zucchini, kernels from corn, tomatoes, slivered garlic, stock, salt and pepper in a microwave-safe bowl.
- Cover, and microwave, stopping and stirring halfway, until the vegetables are tender and the tomatoes have created a broth, 8 to 10 minutes.
- Garnish: Olive oil and basil.

Nutrition Information

- 161: calories;
- 32 grams: carbohydrates;
- 6 grams: dietary fiber;
- 13 grams: sugars;
- 8 grams: protein;
- 1116 milligrams: sodium;
- 3 grams: fat;
- 1 gram: polyunsaturated fat;

---

195.   Vegetable Tostadas With Dark Chili Garlic Sauce

Serving: 4 servings. | Prep: | Cook: | Ready in: 1hours

Ingredients

- For the salsa:
- 2 ancho chilies, stemmed, seeded and deveined (wear rubber gloves to do this)
- 4 garlic cloves, peels on
- 1 canned chipotle chili in adobo, rinsed, stemmed and seeded (wear rubber gloves to do this)
- 1 cup water, more as needed
- 1 tablespoon canola oil
- 1 tablespoon cider vinegar or rice vinegar
- 1 teaspoon sugar
- Salt to taste
- For the tostadas:
- 1 small sweet potato (about 6 ounces), baked
- 1 large carrot (about 6 ounces), peeled and cut in 1/2-inch dice
- 1 medium turnip (about 5 ounces), peeled and cut in 1/2-inch dice
- ¼ pound green beans, cut in 1/2-inch pieces
- ⅔ cup fresh or thawed frozen corn kernels
- 6 corn tortillas, cut in half and toasted in the microwave
- 2 ounces feta cheese or queso fresco, crumbled
- 1 cup thinly shredded cabbage (green or red) or romaine lettuce
- ½ small red or white onion, thinly sliced across the grain (optional)

Direction

- Make the salsa. Place the ancho chilies in a bowl and cover with boiling water. Place a plate on top so that chilies stay submerged. Soak for 30 minutes.
- Meanwhile, toast the garlic cloves in their skins in a dry skillet, stirring, until there are black spots here and there on the skin, the flesh has softened somewhat, and your kitchen smells like toasted garlic. Remove from the heat, allow to cool and remove the skins. Cut away the root end of each clove.
- Drain the soaked chili. Transfer to a blender and add the garlic and chipotle, along with .5 cup of the water. Blend until smooth. Place a strainer over a bowl and strain the sauce.
- Heat a heavy medium saucepan or skillet over medium-high heat and add the oil. Add a spoonful of the purée to see if the pan is hot enough. If it sizzles loudly on contact, pour all of the purée into the pan; if it doesn't, wait a couple of minutes and try again. Cook, stirring, until the sauce thickens and begins to stick to the pan. Add the remaining water, the vinegar, sugar, and salt to taste, and bring to a simmer. Cook, stirring, until the sauce has the consistency of ketchup. Add more water if necessary. Taste, adjust salt, and remove from the heat.
- Steam the carrots, turnips and green beans until tender, about 5 minutes. Add to the sauce along with the sweet potatoes and corn, and stir gently until the vegetables are coated. Heat through in the saucepan and spoon onto the

toasted tortillas. Sprinkle with the cheese, cabbage or lettuce, and optional onions, and serve.

Nutrition Information

- 275: calories;
- 9 grams: sugars;
- 3 grams: monounsaturated fat;
- 0 grams: trans fat;
- 2 grams: polyunsaturated fat;
- 44 grams: carbohydrates;
- 8 grams: protein;
- 771 milligrams: sodium;

196.   Vegetarian Broth

Serving: 6 cups | Prep: | Cook: | Ready in: 1hours15mins

Ingredients

- 1 large tomato, cut in half
- 1 medium-size onion, cut in half
- 1 tablespoon vegetable oil
- 2 medium-size carrots, peeled and cut in 1/2-inch pieces
- ⅓ cup celery leaves
- 1 ½ ounces mushrooms, cut in 1/2-inch pieces
- 1 ounce parsley stems
- 3 medium-size garlic cloves, smashed, peeled and chopped
- 2 ounces cabbage, cut in 1/2-inch slices (optional)
- 1 bay leaf
- Pinch dried thyme
- Pinch dried oregano
- 6 cups water
- 1 ½ teaspoons kosher salt

Direction

- Preheat regular oven to 500 degrees. Coat tomato and onion halves with oil and place in small roasting pan. Cook for about 30 minutes,

gently shaking the pan and turning the vegetables from time to time.

- Place tomato, onion and remaining ingredients except salt in a 5-quart casserole with a tight lid. Cook, covered, at 100 percent power in a high-power oven for 30 minutes.
- Remove from oven and uncover. Strain through a fine sieve and add salt.

Nutrition Information

- 6: calories;
- 83 milligrams: sodium;
- 0 grams: protein;
- 1 gram: carbohydrates;

197.   Walnut Roulade

Serving: 8 servings | Prep: | Cook: | Ready in: 20mins

Ingredients

- 3 eggs, separated
- ⅓ cup granulated sugar
- ½ cup walnuts, finely ground to make 3/4 cup
- ½ teaspoon baking powder
- 1 tablespoon confectioners' sugar
- 1 ½ cups chilled orange curd (see recipe)

Direction

- Line the base of a glass or ceramic dish (14 by 11 by 2 inches) with parchment paper cut to fit. Reserve.
- In a large metal bowl, whisk together egg yolks and granulated sugar until thick and pale. Stir in nuts and baking powder.
- In another bowl, beat egg whites until stiff peaks form. Fold whites into nut mixture until thoroughly mixed. Spread in an even layer on the parchment paper. Cover tightly with microwave plastic wrap. Cook at 100 percent power in a 650- to 700- watt oven for 5 minutes and 30 seconds. Prick plastic to release steam.

- Remove from oven and uncover. Cover loosely with a towel and allow to stand until completely cool.
- Place a larger piece of waxed paper on work surface and sprinkle with confectioner's sugar. When roulade has cooled, turn out onto waxed paper and peel off parchment paper. If not using immediately, roll by lifting the long side of the waxed paper nearest to you and letting the roulade roll on itself, away from you. Cover with plastic wrap and refrigerate.
- When ready to serve, unroll the roulade and spread about 3/4 of the orange curd over the roulade, leaving a 1/4-inch border around the outside. Re-roll the roulade as before and decorate with remaining orange curd.

Nutrition Information

- 112: calories;
- 7 grams: protein;
- 199 milligrams: sodium;
- 4 grams: fat;
- 1 gram: polyunsaturated fat;
- 0 grams: dietary fiber;
- 11 grams: sugars;

198. Watercress Meatloaf

Serving: Four to six servings | Prep: | Cook: | Ready in: 40mins

Ingredients

- 1 pound watercress, stemmed and washed
- 1 medium onion (6 ounces), peeled and quartered
- 3 cloves garlic, smashed and peeled
- 1 ½ cups fresh bread crumbs
- 2 tablespoons tamari soy sauce
- Freshly ground black pepper, to taste
- 1 ½ pounds lean ground beef, preferably top round

Direction

- Place the watercress in a 10-inch pie plate or quiche dish. Cook, uncovered, at 100 percent power for 5 minutes 30 seconds in a microwave oven. Remove from the oven and let stand until cool.
- Place the watercress in a food processor and coarsely chop. Remove to a large mixing bowl. Place the onion and garlic in the food processor and finely chop. Add to the watercress in the mixing bowl, along with the remaining ingredients, and blend well.
- Transfer the mixture to a glass loaf pan measuring 9 by 5 by 3 inches, making sure there are no air pockets. Cover tightly with microwave plastic wrap and cook at 100 percent power for 14 minutes. Prick the plastic to release steam.
- Remove from the oven and uncover. Cover with a kitchen towel and let stand for 10 minutes. Serve hot or cold.

Nutrition Information

- 323: calories;
- 11 grams: fat;
- 4 grams: monounsaturated fat;
- 24 grams: carbohydrates;
- 2 grams: dietary fiber;
- 31 grams: protein;
- 630 milligrams: sodium;
- 1 gram: polyunsaturated fat;
- 3 grams: sugars;

199. White Potato Gratin

Serving: 6 servings | Prep: | Cook: | Ready in: 30mins

Ingredients

- 5 baking potatoes (each 6 to 8 ounces), washed and pricked a few times with a fork
- 1 cup half-and-half

- 6 ounces mozzarella cheese, grated (about 1 1/2 cups)
- 2 ounces grated Parmesan cheese
- Freshly ground black pepper, to taste

Direction

- Arrange potatoes, spoke fashion, on a piece of paper towel in oven. Cook at 100 percent power in a 650-to 700-watt oven for 10 minutes.
- Remove from oven and allow to stand a few minutes. When cool enough to handle, peel with a small sharp knife and cut into 1/4-inch slices.
- Arrange about a third of the potato slices in a glass or ceramic oval dish (13 by 11 by 2 inches). Pour about a third of the half-and-half over the slices, and sprinkle on a third of the cheeses and some black pepper. Repeat layering twice.
- Cook, uncovered, at 100 percent power for 5 minutes.
- Remove from oven and allow to stand, lightly covered with a kitchen towel, for 5 minutes.

Nutrition Information

- 342: calories;
- 15 grams: protein;
- 356 milligrams: sodium;
- 4 grams: monounsaturated fat;
- 1 gram: polyunsaturated fat;
- 3 grams: sugars;
- 14 grams: fat;
- 9 grams: saturated fat;
- 40 grams: carbohydrates;

200.   Wilted Salad Soup

Serving: Two servings | Prep: | Cook: |Ready in: 25mins

Ingredients

- 1 baking potato, about 9 ounces
- 2 tablespoons cornstarch
- 1 ½ cups skim milk
- 1 ⅔ cups wilted salad greens (about 4 cups romaine lettuce leaves and 1/3 cup vinaigrette)
- 1 ½ cups chicken broth
- 1 ½ cups heavy cream
- Coarse salt to taste
- Freshly ground pepper to taste

Direction

- Prick the potato twice with a fork and place in the center of the carousel of a 650- to 700-watt oven. (If your oven does not have a carousel, give the potato a quarter-turn every two minutes.) Cook at 100 percent power for eight minutes. Remove from the oven and cool. Cut the potato in half lengthwise, scoop out the flesh and set aside. Discard the potato skins.
- Combine the cornstarch and milk in a two-and-one-half-quart souffle dish or casserole. Set aside.
- Place the wilted salad in a blender and puree until smooth. Add the reserved potato and the chicken broth and process to combine. Add to the milk mixture. Cover tightly with microwave-safe plastic wrap. Cook at 100 percent power for eight minutes. Prick the plastic to release the steam.
- Remove from the oven and uncover. Stir in the cream, salt and pepper and serve.

Nutrition Information

- 861: calories;
- 20 grams: monounsaturated fat;
- 3 grams: polyunsaturated fat;
- 2 grams: dietary fiber;
- 18 grams: sugars;
- 42 grams: saturated fat;
- 69 grams: fat;
- 47 grams: carbohydrates;
- 17 grams: protein;
- 1654 milligrams: sodium;

- 6 grams: fat;
- 0 grams: polyunsaturated fat;
- 3 grams: dietary fiber;

201. Yummy Bananas

Serving: Four servings | Prep: | Cook: | Ready in: 10mins

Ingredients

- ⅓ cup dark or light brown sugar
- 2 tablespoons unsalted butter
- 1 2-inch piece vanilla bean or 1/2 teaspoon vanilla extract
- 2 thin slices fresh ginger
- 2 tablespoons fresh orange juice
- 4 small, just-ripe bananas, 5 to 6 ounces each, peeled

Direction

- Place the sugar, butter, vanilla bean if using and ginger in a 10-inch pie plate or quiche dish. Cover tightly with microwave plastic wrap. Cook at 100 percent power in a 650- to 700-watt microwave oven for 2 minutes. Prick the plastic to release steam.
- Remove from the oven and uncover. Remove the vanilla bean and ginger and stir in the orange juice. If using vanilla extract, add it now. Arrange the bananas in the dish, pinwheel fashion, and spoon over the sauce. Cover tightly with microwave plastic wrap and cook for 3 minutes. Prick the plastic to release steam.
- Remove from the oven, uncover and serve warm over ice cream or with whipped cream.

Nutrition Information

- 193: calories;
- 36 grams: carbohydrates;
- 25 grams: sugars;
- 1 gram: protein;
- 5 milligrams: sodium;
- 4 grams: saturated fat;
- 2 grams: monounsaturated fat;

202. Zucchini Confit

Serving: | Prep: | Cook: | Ready in: 10mins

Ingredients

- 1 ½ pounds of zucchini
- ¼ cup butter or olive oil, or both
- Salt and pepper, for seasoning
- Parsley for garnish

Direction

- Cut 1 1/2 pounds zucchini crosswise into 1/2-inch pieces, put in a microwave-safe bowl with 1/4 cup butter or olive oil or both, season with salt and pepper and microwave, covered, stirring halfway, until tender, 4 to 6 minutes.
- Garnish: Parsley.

Nutrition Information

- 150: calories;
- 14 grams: fat;
- 2 grams: protein;
- 10 grams: monounsaturated fat;
- 6 grams: carbohydrates;
- 4 grams: sugars;
- 428 milligrams: sodium;

Index

Conclusion

Thank you again for downloading this book!

I hope you enjoyed reading about my book!

If you enjoyed this book, please take the time to share your thoughts and post a review on Amazon. It'd be greatly appreciated!

Write me an honest review about the book – I truly value your opinion and thoughts and I will incorporate them into my next book, which is already underway.

Thank you!

If you have any questions, **feel free to contact at:** _author@tarragonrecipes.com_

Mary Solomon

tarragonrecipes.com

Printed in Great Britain
by Amazon